What's In the Way IS the Way

Moving Beyond Your Struggle into the Joy of Being *Fully* Alive

By Mary O'Malley

Awaken Publications

Kirkland, Washington

©2013

Dedication

This book is dedicated to MarySue Brooks, my treasured friend and business partner. Thank you for living this work and bringing your wisdom to it. Your presence, your skills, your commitment and your heart have been necessary in its unfolding. Words cannot describe how grateful I am that we get to walk this path together.

∞

Acknowledgments

It takes a village to birth a book! Besides MarySue, there have been countless others who have supported this work. I host four ongoing groups which have been the incubators of the essence of what is being offered here and I thank each and every person who has been, is right now or will be a part of one of the groups. This is also true of everybody I have worked with on an individual basis for healing happens when two people show up together in curiosity and compassion.

I also thank my children Katrina and Micah for doing such a good job in raising me. I grew with, for and because of them!

My dear friend Stephanie Kerns is an essential part of this unfolding. Not only has she been my retreat manager, but it is with her that I learned the art of true friendship.

I also feel deep gratitude for the people who have supported this book: Mark Ricker, who keeps our computers in top form; Kai Openshaw who knows English a lot better than I do; Ginny Howell who gave excellent feedback on the content of the book; the two in-person groups who lived the Re-membering Sessions and helped to fine tune them; and finally Rhett Reynolds who was the last proof-reader and whose eagle eyes were essential in catching mistakes.

I

Table of Contents

Foreword

When I was a boy, I used to go around saying, "Life is so simple. Why does everyone keep making it so complicated?"

I couldn't understand why all the kids in school would get so kerfuffled when a big test was coming up, or when the end-of-year grades were due. I couldn't figure out (even when I was 7, 8, and 9) why Mom and Dad "got into it" so often at home, or why my Mom worried so much about stuff.

I was never clear about why anyone would be so concerned or worried about anything that they'd let themselves shift from cheerfulness to snippiness, from happiness to grouchiness, from inner peace to inward anxiety.

For some reason, I always knew things would work out—and they always did. Maybe they didn't always work out the way I thought they would, or exactly the way I wanted them to, but they always worked out in a way that brought me to my next highest good—and it didn't take me long to catch on to what was happening, and to begin to depend on this being simply "The Way Life Is."

Now wonderful spiritual teacher Mary O'Malley has written a whole book about this—explaining it clearly, and in wonderfully accessible terms.

I'm so excited about this book! I consider it to be one of the most important pieces of writing to come our way in a very long time, and it absolutely will be—of this I am sure—one of the most beneficial books you have ever read.

This book talks about how to deal with life exactly as it is occurring, not just when it's easy to do so, but when it's the most difficult—which, irony of ironies, makes it easy to do so.

And as much as I thought I knew about all this, boy, could I have used this book when I was moving through the worst days of my personal journey. As with all of us, there have been some pretty tough ones. And in those moments we can easily forget—or, at least, I did—whatever we thought we knew about how to navigate the rocky shoals of life.

If in those moments I could have had something that I could turn to, something that could have helped me understand what was going on and how to get through it, I would have given anything. And if I had had something that I could refer to ahead of time so that I might have a specific approach to dealing with challenging moments, I would have considered it the biggest blessing of my life.

I can promise you that you will never find life more clearly explained than it is here, nor will you have placed in your hands more useful or powerful tools with which to negotiate its most difficult experiences.

It is true for me that as a child I seemed to know, intuitively, that life need not be as utterly discombobulating as I was observing people experiencing it, but I could not have told you why that was so—much less how to make it so. Mary O'Malley has done both here, and thus produced one of the greatest gifts one human being could offer to another.

If this is a challenging time in your life (or if someone you know and love is moving through a challenging moment in theirs), you could not have been led to a more perfect resource than this book—nor a more compassionate, understanding, spiritually aware, emotionally articulate, psychologically brilliant, and wonderfully able and capable messenger and teacher than its author.

Put simply, this book will show you the way to a better life, without needing a single thing to be different for you to retain your inner peace, your outer joy, and your overall well-being. Yet it is far from a theory book, or a concept document. It is a Practitioner's Guide. It is an easy-to-follow Instruction Book. It could easily have been titled Life's Operating Manual.

Your soul knew exactly what it was doing when it brought you here. (You know, of course, that you did not "stumble upon" this book by chance.) Absorb it, then. Inhale it. Drink it in as the nectar of the gods. For it is surely from Divinity Itself that flows such wisdom as is here.

Thank you Mary O'Malley, for our days and nights are enriched by you, and our wounded places healed.

Neale Donald Walsch
Author *Conversations with God*

Introduction

Your Transformation Begins

I am inviting you on the most important journey you will ever take: the journey back to a heartfelt connection with yourself and a trust-filled connection with your life. This journey will show you that there is a sense of well-being with you always, ***no matter what is happening in your life***.

If you are like most people, you only have sporadic glimpses of the well-being that is your birthright. This may be because you, like most everyone else, have a deep belief inside of you that says you are not *enough*. You may also have been conditioned to believe that if you just fix yourself or your life, you will be enough and thus know the peace you long for. So you have become an ongoing project, believing that if you just get yourself and your life to be a particular way, then you will be happy. This causes you to struggle with your compulsions, your finances, your relationships, and your health. Rather than peace and joy, you may very well be living in a low grade sense of unease that periodically flares up and plunges you into turmoil. So your life has become a series of problems to be solved rather than an adventure to be lived!

If you are honest with yourself, you would recognize that this fixing game has never brought you the deep healing you long for. But don't despair. There is another way to live that will permeate your life with well-being. This is what we will be exploring together in this book.

It is important for you to understand that I too lived from this place of struggle for many years, so I intimately know the deep pain and heartache that comes from the fix-it mode. I was very compulsive, at times suicidal, and felt that I had no value. Most of the time, I experienced a sense of unease, and oftentimes it would flare up into dread and hopeless despair. These feelings would show up as relentless struggles in my head. They also appeared as an overall anxiousness that created knots in my stomach and debilitating headaches that came from an intense longing to run away from my life. I gained a huge amount of weight, washed a lot of the food down with alcohol, and took every pill I could get my hands on.

Since I perceived myself as defective, I tried to get rid of the parts of me I didn't like and hold onto the ones I did. But these parts seemed to have a life of their own, appearing when I didn't want them to be here and disappearing when I wanted them to stay. I also desperately tried to understand it all, but that just kept me caught in my head.

It wasn't until I discovered how to listen to myself that I began to open up again. Rather than always being in fix-it mode, I learned how to meet myself exactly as I am, opening into the place beyond judging, fixing, getting rid of, and trying to understand. I learned that listening is the art of being present for my own experience, no matter what it is. Most of all, it is the art of meeting myself in my own heart – even the so-called unacceptable, unmeetable parts.

Slowly, just as the morning light dispels the dark, I came back to myself and back to Life. Rather than being in a constant state of unease, I came to know more and more joy, trust and love. I also discovered how to show up for the great adventure called Life – not an idea of what it should be, but the real thing. Rather than always trying to create a better reality, I showed up for Reality!

Did this make all of my vulnerabilities go away? No. These feelings will always be a part of me, for vulnerability is an essential part of being human, and vulnerabilities hold the doorways back into the peace, joy and love that is our birthright. Now mine are nestled in the spaciousness of my own heart. And when they get reawakened through this sometimes fierce process called Life, they don't take over any more. Instead, they open my heart even more.

This is the journey that I am inviting you on – the journey back to the ease and well-being you long for. On this journey, you will discover how to heal the game of struggle, so you can know the joy of being *fully* alive. You will also learn how to meet yourself exactly as you are, weaving every part of yourself into your own heart – even the parts you think are unlikable and unlovable. It will become clear as you read this book that you can also move beyond being a victim to the challenges of your life so you can gather the treasures that always come with them. And finally, you will rediscover how to be open to Life again, right here, right now, feeling at home no matter where you are, no matter what is happening All of this will bring you to the place of knowing the safety of showing up for the great adventure called Life – not an idea of what it should be, but the real thing, so your heart can sing!

The first step in this journey back to being *fully* awake to Life is a radical shift of your perception. The field of well-being you long for is here right now as you are reading this book! You don't need to search for it; you don't need to fix yourself to know it; and you don't even need to change anything in your life. Your innate sense of well-being is revealed as you learn how to unhook from your struggling self.

In this book, you will discover that struggle is like a cloud bank of stories that cuts you off from your natural state of joy and peace, and you have been conditioned throughout your life to believe in these stories. Struggle is based on fear; it is held together with judgment, and it leaves you vulnerable to sadness, loneliness and despair. Your struggling self doesn't only grapple with the big challenges of Life; it also resists the smaller things, like the length of the stoplight, the spot on your shirt, or the shape of your nose.

As you work with what is being offered in this book, you will discover how not to get seduced by your mind's addiction to struggle. Step-by-step, you will learn how you became caught in struggle; how to see the particular stories of struggle you were conditioned to believe; and how to give them the spacious acceptance they need to be healed. Through the power of your own focused attention, your struggles will dissipate, just as the morning fog lifts under the gaze of the sun.

You will also come to see that your life, rather than being a series of events that are happening to you, is all happening for you. Everything in your life – especially your challenges – is tailor-made to help you see your stories of struggle. So whatever is in the way is the way! Rather than struggling with your challenges, you will learn how to listen to them so they can heal you to your core.

As you deepen into this process, you will discover how to unhook from all of the fears, longings, irritations, and sorrows that struggle generates. Rather than getting seduced into struggle or turning to your compulsions or fighting with the people in your life, you will be able to simply let it all pass through you, discovering that at any given moment only a small part of you has a problem with Life. The rest of you is at peace. That is the field of well-being that is always with you right here, right now.

This is what you deeply long for – an intimate connection with Life. At your core, you yearn to show up for what Life is offering in this moment rather than wanting your experience to be different than it is. You long to let go of trying, resisting, and constantly evaluating how you are doing, so you can relax into your life and know the joy of being *fully* available and present for Life.

Understanding what is being offered here is an important step, but it won't of itself open the doors into the healing you long for. This happens through experiencing what is being offered here. So throughout this book, you will be invited with this symbol -Ω- to pause and open to Life, connecting with what is being offered in that moment.

Also, I have designed the book as a ten week introspective process, although it is okay to go at your own pace. This process is found in the Re-membering Section at the end of each chapter. There you will be given a Re-membering Statement that embodies the essence of the chapter which you can use to help reconnect with what you are exploring that week. There is also a space for you to write your own statement.

Then, through a Re-membering Session, you will be encouraged to spend some time with yourself every day, learning how to see and listen to your inner experiences rather than being seduced by the game of struggle. In each chapter, we will build upon what we explored in the previous chapter. Finally, there will be a list of the main points called Re-memberings at the end of each chapter, and I encourage you to add your own if that calls to you. This list will be helpful in keeping the shifts of perception that are happening as you go through this process in the forefront of your awareness.

Are you ready to step out of the box of struggle and come back to the joy of being *fully* alive? You may have some resistance to this for we all deeply long to be open to Life again, but we are also afraid of it. So, it is important to remember that what I am offering you here comes from having actually lived it. Rather than staying lost in the depth of darkness I took on, Life showed me the pathway from contraction and struggle to connection and well-being. Since I began sharing my pathway, I have guided thousands of people over the last 30 years to discover their journey back to themselves and back to Life. Furthermore, each of them helped me to see more clearly the pathway back to Life.

So, if your answer is yes to the journey from struggle to well-being, let's begin.

And for all the people that live on this beautiful blue-green jewel that is our planet, I thank you for your willingness to bring this process into your life. This gratitude comes from knowing that, as you discover and live from your field of well-being, your life will be transformed. You will also transform the lives of everybody you meet, and even think about, for the rest of your life. For when you are not caught in the world of struggle, you are here, open to the amazing majesty and mystery of Life, radiating the presence of well-being. And a human being who has discovered how to be here becomes an invitation to all beings to unhook from the mind's addiction to struggle and open back into the joy of being *fully* here for Life.

For the healing of all beings, Life is bringing you home.

Mary O'Malley

What's in the Way IS the Way

CHAPTER 1:

It's All Okay – It's Truly Okay

Imagine a day where everything was okay; not only okay but really okay. You may have just fallen in love; or you received something you have wanted for a long time; or you're on vacation with no pressures, lying on a beach in deep contentment. Allow the images of your okay day to fill you up. Go for the gusto – let that *okayness* in. Let it flood your mind, your body and your heart.

Now notice what you are experiencing as you use your imagination to open up to the joy of everything being okay. In your mind there is probably a sense that nothing needs to be any different than it is. In your body, there is an experience of deep relaxation that allows for the glow of joy. And your heart is open, spacious and light. Ahh.

What would it be like if you knew that everything was always okay? That doesn't mean there wouldn't be challenges. It just means that you wouldn't turn them into problems so then you would be able to respond to them from a clear place. What would it be like to live from this open, relaxed, engaged and spacious place? Isn't this what you deeply long for – to no longer struggle with Life and instead be available to the experience of Life as it is right here, right now? This is possible! In fact everything in your Life is a part of the journey into recognizing and living from a place that is beyond struggle.

The Myth of Not Being Okay:

We all long for this *okayness* and yet it seems very illusive. If you step back and look at what is going on inside of you all day long, you would see that rather than resting in the ease of *okayness*, your mind is oftentimes doing the opposite. It is searching for something better – a better body, a better mate, a better meditation, a better car, a better mind. This kind of mind hopes that if you can just get your life the way you want it to be, then you will feel okay.

You can also spend a lot of energy trying to get rid of the parts of you that you don't like. You hope all of this wanting and resisting will finally soothe the raging beast of the voice in your head that says you and your life need to be different than what they are in order to have everything be okay. When struggling with your life doesn't bring you the lasting satisfaction you long for, you then look for it through the numbing world of compulsions.

When you look honestly at your search for a better experience, you will see that it doesn't work! Or the better way to say it is that it does work - for brief moments – but this only keeps you caught in the belief that if you just do it right – if you change yourself and your life enough -then you will know that illusive *okayness* you so deeply long for. But haven't you noticed that every time your mind feels that it has gotten it all together it hasn't stayed that way?

It is very important to understand that the mind is not being put down here. It is an exquisite creation of Life that took 14 billion years to form. Life created it as a tool for maneuvering through Life – not to be in charge of it. It is a wonderful servant but it is a horrible master. Giving it the task of being in charge of Life has created the world of struggle that most people live in all day long, keeping them cut off from the peace and joy they long for.

The more you can learn how to use your mind rather than having it use you, you discover that the *okayness* you long for is your natural state and it is always with you no matter what is happening in your life. You just don't see it because you are always trying to find it! And you can't find it, for you have never lost it. You could be angry, or deeply despairing, or even very afraid, and your natural field of well-being is also there at the same moment you are caught in struggle! You can learn how to recognize and live from the place beyond struggle, no matter what is happening in your life.

As we explore the doorways back into your natural *okayness*, there will be invitations throughout the book to let go of the world of struggle and open to Life here and now. Whenever you see this sign, -Ω-, it is an invitation to take some time to dip the finger of your attention into the river of your experience and let Life in. This is essential for there are a lot of words in this book, and you can stay at just the level of words, but the deep healing you long for happens when you can feel what is being offered here. You don't have to figure out what that is – you simply discover that you can let go of the game of struggle and connect with Life right now.

-Ω- Close your eyes for a moment and listen to your life. There are all sorts of sounds happening right now. To keep your mind engaged, count how many different sounds you can hear. When you are done, open your eyes and recognize something very amazing. For a moment your intention wasn't to think about Life. It was to directly experience it by listening to it. There is a big difference between thinking about Life and actually experiencing it.

The Meadow:

There is a metaphor that will clarify what we are exploring here. Imagine a beautiful meadow on a sunlit morning. In this meadow is a rainbow of wildflowers, along with the heart-opening music of birds. The smells of the heather and the pristine beauty of the surrounding mountains all bring forth a deep sense of peace.

This meadow represents the experience of *okayness* that is at the heart of Life. You knew this *okayness* when you were very young. You may have no memories of this kind of well-being but there was a time when there were no thoughts in your head. Past and future had no meaning for you, so this moment was all there was. Because you weren't searching for a better state, you were open to it – all of it – and Life was okay exactly as it was. Even when there was pain and discomfort, you fully experienced it rather than turning it into a problem in your mind.

Now imagine yourself as a young child living in the meadow, fascinated by the newness of every moment, open to everything. Clouds come and go as do laughter and tears, so everything inside of you and outside of you flows. As you grew, thoughts began to fill your head as you started to tell yourself stories about yourself and about Life.

Now imagine the clouds in the sky beginning to circle around your head.

At first they were just wispy clouds that didn't fully block your experience of the meadow. But overtime, usually by adolescence, the clouds completely surround and fill your head, so much so that you could no longer see the meadow. All you could see were the ever-shifting clouds of your mind.

This is where most people live, caught in the cloud banks of their minds, lost in ideas about Life rather than the direct experience of it. When you first saw a bird when you were young, you saw it in all of its mystery. You experienced it not as an object of your mind but as a living experience all throughout your being. As you grew up, you began to experience it as a thought – oh that is a bird. Your thoughts about Life make up the cloud bank of your mind that separates you from Life.

At this point it may be difficult for you to see that you are lost in a cloud bank because it has been awhile since you have spent an extended period of time in the ease and joy of the meadow of your being. So you, like most people, became used to chronic, low grade struggles, believing that your thoughts were true and if you could only get them to be the way you want them to be, then everything would be okay. This only leads to endless struggle.

The Storyteller:

These clouds that fill up your mind are made up of all of the stories you have learned to tell yourself about yourself and about Life. You know what I mean – the storyteller in your head that talks all day. Your storyteller is the voice of your cloud bank of struggle. If you had a little door on your forehead that you could open up and watch the storyteller, you would see it voices an opinion about everything – it comments on what it likes and what it doesn't like. It tells you what you should do and shouldn't do and oftentimes changes from one to the other in a matter of seconds! It judges unmercifully, not only other people but also yourself. And it is afraid – afraid of Life, afraid of its own fear and deeply afraid of being alone.

Because the storyteller is constantly trying to do it right it manipulates, tries, expects, wants, rages and resists. It generates all sorts of feelings such as fear, sadness, self-judgment, anger, doubt, confusion, irritation and despair, to name a few. It also generates feelings of love, kindness, and peace but these usually only show up when the storyteller is getting what it wants. As soon as it doesn't, any feelings that generate from the heart are usually closed down.

Most of the stories in your head struggle with everyday things like the length of the line at the grocery store, the color of your new makeup, your mate changing the channel, you gained two pounds. But at times it also flares up into big struggles, such as: "He rejected me and I can't stand to be alone." "I found a lump in my breast and I am going to die." "If I don't get a job, I will lose my house and will have to live on the streets." It is very good at *awfulizing*, leaving you in contraction and reaction, unable to respond to the challenges of your life in a clear way.

The storyteller comes from being disconnected from Life. It comes from believing you are separate from the meadow and thus have to *do* life rather than *be* Life. I am not putting down thought. It is an exquisite tool for maneuvering through reality, but your thoughts are not reality. They are not the meadow. They are just ideas about the meadow and they have a tendency to react to life rather than respond to it.

Now imagine an alien arriving from another planet and landing beside this meadow. He sees you standing there fighting with your clouds, trying to make them be different or to have them just go away. As he watches you struggle, he notices that your clouds become thicker and you have times where you become frozen, lost in despair. This confuses the alien because he can clearly see that you are struggling with nothing more substantial than clouds. On top of that, he can see that you are standing in the meadow of peace you are so desperately trying to find; you just don't recognize it!

The core of what is being offered here (and will be said over and over again because our cloud banks can seem so thick) is: *the meadow of well-being is always with you!* You usually don't notice it because you have been conditioned to only pay attention to the stories in your head. And if you watch closely, you will see that the storyteller is lost in an endless game of struggle – the game that says if you just get yourself and your life to be the way you think they should be, then the peace you long for will be here.

But this will never bring you the lasting peace that is your natural state. You can win the lottery, think happy thoughts until the cows come home; meditate for hours every day in order to find the states of mind you like; do enough plastic surgery to make your body be what you think is perfect, and still, in the long run, none of that is enough because *all of these things are not the meadow.* They are just attempts to find the meadow and they will only thicken your cloud bank in the long run.

Everything you long for and everything you truly are is to be found right here in the meadow of *this moment.* You access the meadow through simply being open to Life. Being open is having a direct experience with whatever you are experiencing **no matter what is happening**, including the easy and the difficult, the joyous and the sorrowful. In other words, it is about discovering how to show up for the Life you have been given rather than endlessly trying to have it be different than what it is.

-Ω- Open to the possibility that you are in the meadow right now as you are reading this book.

The Meadow of Your Heart:

It is an amazing awakening when you realize you have been chasing pleasant states your whole life and resisting the unpleasant ones, and this has never brought you the peace you long for! Rather than searching for 'the ultimate experience of your life,' how would it feel to settle into the flow of Life enough so every experience is 'the experience of my life!' (even the difficult). This radical acceptance opens you to the meadow of your being – no matter what is happening.

It is your heart that knows how to be open to it all. When you are caught in the cloud bank of struggle, you experience your life only through your mind that clings and resists. When you thin your cloud bank enough, you begin to experience life through your heart, which is the doorway into the meadow.

It is important to expand our definition of the heart beyond the fairly limited view that permeates our culture. Both the ancient wisdom of Ayurvedic medicine and the modern science of Heart Math understand that the core of your being is the heart - not the physical organ, but the energy essence of the heart. Your heart, rather than your mind, is the source of wisdom, healing and love and it is very smart. It is the heart that can feel Life, connecting with it through resonance. It knows how to include rather than exclude; to accept rather than judge; to allow rather than resist. Your experience of life is completely different when you learn how to feel your way with your heart rather than thinking about it with your mind.

You lived in an open heart when you were very young but, like most people, you were scared out of it. In order to not continually suffer the pain of a broken heart, you ran away to your head. You were like Sleeping Beauty pricking your finger on the spindle of your thoughts, falling asleep to healing power of your heart.

But you, like Sleeping Beauty, can wake up again. You can let your heart open again and discover that it is the wisest guide and friend you will ever have. As you discover how to listen to it and trust it, it will become a doorway into the meadow of Life. Your heart is the gatekeeper for the energy of aliveness that you really are, and the more closed it is, the more depressed you feel, cut off from the flow of Life. The more open it is, the more you have access to your natural state of love– no matter what is happening.

Your heart is not just about feelings. It is literally an energy center that resides in your chest and when it is open, it fills your whole being with its wisdom energy. Pull up a memory of someone you deeply care for and allow yourself to really feel how much you care. If you watch carefully you will see that the energy in your chest opens up. Now call up a time where you were angry and reactive. Notice that the energy in your chest closes down. Now pull up the first memory and allow your heart to glow again.

It is possible to live a life in which your reactive mind does not close down the wisdom of your heart, and this is what this journey we are on is all about. When you have seen through your cloud bank enough that your heart feels safe to open again, rather than being an object in your mind, Life becomes the subject of your heart. Every single part of you - even the so called unacceptable parts – is woven back into your heart. Also, rather than experiencing people through your wanting and resisting mind, you experience them through your heart – even difficult people.

-Ω- Bring your attention to the center of your chest and breathe in and out through your heart center. If you have never done this before, imagine breathing through a little nose in the center of your chest. Now see at the center of your chest a tiny flame, and every time you breathe in, the flame becomes brighter.

The Power of Compassionate Curiosity:

How do you reconnect? How do you discover the meadow of your heart rather than living in the reactions of your mind? It isn't about trying to get back to the meadow – that is just more struggle. Besides, you have never left the meadow; you just think you have. Rather than trying to get rid of your cloud bank, the key is getting to know it. It isn't about trying to fix it, change it or get rid of it. It is about learning how to be curious about what is going on in your life, both inside of you and outside, so you can see what the storyteller is doing inside your head. The more you look, the less you take these stories personally, and it becomes easier and easier to unhook from them.

Imagine being so lost in a wave of fear that your mind is whirling and there is a tightly held fist in your stomach. Then imagine curiosity kicking in. You notice that your belly is tight and your mind is spinning. Rather than falling into the fear, you can be with it. "This is just fear and I can be curious about it." In that moment, rather than being lost in your mind's resistance to what you are experiencing, you have instead turned your attention toward what is actually happening – not an idea of it, but the living experience of it.

To reconnect with *what is* is to make contact with what you are actually experiencing before you think about it. This may not seem very powerful, but it is. Instead of being caught in the clouds of fear, you have stepped back and have *related to* fear rather than being lost in it. Your ability to be aware of what is going on inside of you may last for just a moment before the clouds of fear take over again, but that moment matters! This ability to see what your mind is doing rather than being lost in it is an important step in learning how to unhook from the game of struggle that runs most people's minds.

This ability to be curious about what you are experiencing opens you to the place where lasting healing happens. This is where you discover how to meet all of your stories and the feelings they generate with the wisdom of your heart. If you are like most people, you are either ashamed of or afraid of the stories that make up your cloud bank, so you hide them deep inside. If they do make it to the surface of your awareness, you judge yourself for having them and then you spend your energy trying to ignore them or get rid of them. But they are just like people. They react when they are judged and they let go when they are listened to.

You can learn how to bring compassionate curiosity to all of the stories in your head. The more you bring the light of your compassionate attention to the stories you have been caught in most of your life, the more they thin like clouds thin when touched by the warmth of the sun. Not only do they thin, they become doorways back into the meadow which is the place where no matter what is happening in your life, everything is okay.

> -Ω- Take a moment to listen to Life again. Notice that the sounds are different than when you listened a few pages ago. In these few moments you are using your mind to be curious about Life rather than just thinking about it.

What's in the Way IS the Way:

The more curious you are about what you are experiencing rather than constantly trying to change it, the more you discover an amazing truth - you naturally know how to show up for your life, partnering with Life rather than always trying to change it. You also see that no object, person or experience will ever bring you the deep and lasting peace that comes from learning how to simply be open to Life. You then become less interested in trying to create your reality and more willing to show up for Life as it is unfolding.

This shift of perception comes from the understanding that Life is *for* you. It is very difficult, if not impossible, to see this truth when you are caught in the cloud bank of your separate self. We will be exploring this in more depth towards the end of the book, but know that the more your cloud bank thins, the more you can see that Life is trustable. It is not always likable, but *what's in the way IS the way* and it can be trusted. Trust is not trusting that you will get what you *want*. Trust understands that you will get what you *need* in order to come out of the cloud bank of struggle. So trust doesn't just trust the easy. It also trusts the difficult. Trust knows that the challenges of your life are for you. They are the yellow highlighter of Life showing you the clouds of your reactive mind so that you can thin them with the sunlight of your own attention and thus rediscover the meadow of this moment.

The more compassionate curiosity develops inside of you and brings you to your natural state of trust, the more you will be able to relax, allowing Life to flow through you rather than resisting or trying to hold onto it. Your life then becomes an adventure and every moment is either an invitation to be engaged with the joy of being fully alive or Life is putting you in the situations that bring up the stories of your cloud bank so they can be thinned. The more they thin, the more your energy opens up. The more you open up the more you connect and this is what we all deeply long for.

Joseph Campbell, the much-loved mythologist and writer, said it very well, "People say that what we're all seeking is a meaning for Life. I don't think that's what we're really seeking. I think what we're seeking is an experience of being alive, so that our life experiences on the purely physical plane will have resonance within our own innermost being and reality, so that we actually feel the rapture of being alive. That's what it's all finally about."

What Campbell is alluding to is at the heart of this book. It is an invitation to fully experience Life so you can again know *the rapture of being alive*, which is all about connecting with what is right here, right now, before thinking takes over. We will be going on a ten week adventure together thinning the cloud banks of our minds and opening into the meadow of our hearts. This adventure will help you rediscover the power of your own attentive heart that can dispel your clouds, allowing you to re-member that the meadow of your own being is always with you right here, right now.

In Chapter Two we will explore the qualities of the meadow. In Chapter Three we will look at fear which is the core movement of your storyteller and discover that it is possible to see through its stories. Before we learn the art of being curious about our immediate experience, in Chapter Four we take the essential step of discovering that you are not the one in charge of this process - that you are not alone and help is only a question away.

With this foundation, we will then explore in Chapter Five the power of being curious about your immediate experience. In Chapter Six you will discover how to bring the power of curiosity into your daily life. In Chapter Seven we will look at your hearts ability to heal. Then in Chapter Eight you will learn how to touch even the deepest of holdings inside of you with the healing of your heart.

In Chapter Nine you will reconnect with your natural state of trust. In Chapter 10, all that we have explored will be brought together into four guidelines that will help you to be with whatever Life brings you. In Chapter 11, you will discover that what we are exploring here has the power to transform the world.

The core of our journey together is about opening what has been closed inside of you so that the energy that has been bound up in your cloud bank of struggle can be released and you can again know the joy of being fully alive.

> -Ω- Let go of all that we have been exploring here and connect with Life. Use whatever senses are calling to you to make direct contact with Life. Hear it, see it, touch it, feel it coursing through your body. This is a brand new moment in your life. You have never experienced this moment before and will never again. The quality of light is different; the sensations in your body are different; even the sounds you are hearing are brand new. There is an intelligent flow going on here, a flow that you can consciously enter through the wisdom of your heart. Whether it is for two seconds or ten minutes, stay with this as long as it interests you and then resume reading.

RE-MEMBERING SECTION

At the end of each chapter, there will be a Re-membering Section which includes a Re-membering Statement that sums up what we have explored in this chapter, a Re-membering Session that will help you bring the essence of the chapter into your daily life, and core Re-memberings with bullets that summarize the chapter.

Re-membering Statement

The Re-membering Statement captures the essence of what we have explored in the chapter. These truths come from the meadow – the place beyond the struggling self. They will help you, as you move throughout your day, to reconnect with what we are exploring that week.

You can write them on sticky notes and place them around your life. Or you can connect them with something you do many times a day, such as using the bathroom or answering the phone. You can even use them as a mantra during your times of conscious breathing.

These truths will also be helpful in getting to know your struggling self for it may at times argue with the core re-membering. Notice when your mind is open to it and notice what it says when it is not. Also, remember that when it is arguing with the statement, this is just the cloud bank of struggle.

If the statement that is chosen for the week doesn't call to you, ask yourself what touched you the most in the chapter. Then put it in a few words that you can come back to throughout the week, reminding yourself what you are re-membering.

This week's Re-membering Statement:

Right now, this is Life and it's okay.

Your Own Statement:

_____

Re-membering Session

You are invited to spend some time every day bringing what we are exploring into your immediate experience. I call this dipping the finger of your attention into the river of your experience. This may look like meditation but, in the traditional sense, it is not. Rather than trying to make something happen, or get to a better state, or trying to change what is, you are strengthening the muscle of your attention. With attention, you can be curious about what is going on right now in order to discover how to relate to your immediate experience rather than turning it into a problem. For it is when your attention and your immediate experience come together that the cloud bank lifts and you rediscover the meadow.

Your Re-membering Session is a powerful place to get to know the cloud bank of your mind. If you are like most people, your mind will have times when it struggles with the sessions. It will try to do it and do it right, judging itself for how it is doing. It will oftentimes get bored or just space out. This is why most people think they are failures at what is called meditation for they are trying to do it right. But your experience would be completely different if you knew that whatever shows up in your daily sessions is exactly what needs to be there and when you can be curious about it, you step out of the game of struggle.

For the first few weeks you will be invited into the amazing world of your breath which will become a sanctuary that you can return to when you get caught in the cloud bank of your mind. As you learn how to truly experience your own breath, you will drift off into the storyteller in your head over and over again. Your storyteller will get impatient, confused, spaced out. Your attention will get caught in stories about the future and will drift off into the past. Of course your mind will wander for you have been lost in thought for most of your life.

No need to make this a problem. Each time you drift off, it is an opportunity to see that you are no longer aware of your breath. Each time you bring your attention back, you will have strengthened the muscle of your attention! You may be able to catch this after just a few moments or it may be ten minutes. It doesn't matter. No judgment here for how much you leave your breath. As the muscle of your attention strengthens, you will then be shown step-by-step how to see your cloud bank of struggle, rather than identifying with it, so it can begin to thin and eventually lift.

If you have spent time with yourself, explore for as long as you are interested. For those of you who have never spent time quietly and intimately being with yourself, we will start with five minutes a day and add a minute a week. You may want to set the timer on your phone (with a gentle ring). Also, if on a particular day, the amount of time for that week is too much for you, trust that and shorten your time a bit. Consistency is much more important than length of time.

Even with this short period of time, your mind may resist giving you this gift of your own attention. It may say, "You don't have time" or "It's self-indulgent" or "You won't do it right." One of its favorites is to get bored because your attention has been so used to the busy world of your thoughts. It may also try to figure things out or get lost in wanting your immediate experience to be different than what it is.

All of this is just the cloud bank of struggle. Hold the intention to give yourself this time and then notice what the mind does with it. If resistance to giving yourself this gift takes over, be curious about resistance. Isn't it amazing that you are resistant to spending just a few minutes of quality time with yourself?

It is important as you learn the art of being with your own experience to let go of judging how you are doing. If you turned your attention toward yourself for five minutes and you were truly curious for maybe two moments, that is time well spent because those moments strengthen the muscle of your attention. The stronger your muscle becomes, the more you will be able to be present for whatever is happening. Then Life can pass through and you can again know the joy of being alive.

For many people it is usually helpful to connect with yourself in this way as early in the day as you can so it sets a tone for the day. But if this doesn't work for you, find a time during the day when you can regularly set aside time to explore the Re-membering Session of the week.

You can also sprinkle a minute or two of becoming curious about what you are experiencing as you move throughout your day. It can help to connect this with something you do a number of times during the day like eating, using the bathroom or answering the phone.

On the first day of each week, read through the instructions for that chapter and then close your eyes and go exploring. The abbreviated version at the end of the instructions will guide you after that.

Let us now strengthen the muscle of your attention so you can discover how to be present for your own experience. We will start through relaxing the chronic holding in your body and then we will bring your attention to the circle of your breath.

Find a comfortable spot where you won't be interrupted by people, phones or animals. Begin by closing your eyes and taking a moment to recognize that all of the millions of moments of your life have brought you to this moment and this moment is unique. You are not watching television, taking a shower or eating your breakfast. You are sitting, with your eyes closed, with the intention to become curious about what you are experiencing right now. Notice what you can notice about this moment of your life.

On the next in-breath, tighten your muscles. Tighten, tighten, tighten. Then slowly, very slowly, relax everything on your out-breath as you say the great sound of letting go, "Ahh!" Feel the deliciousness of deeply letting go, coupled with the power of "Ahh." Play with this sound as there are many different ways you can express it. This melts the chronic holding you carry around in your body/mind all day long. (If you are in a place where it is uncomfortable to make sounds, say it silently to yourself.) Do this for at least three breaths.

Now allow your breath to be as it wants to be and be curious about how different an in-breath is from an out-breath. An in-breath lifts and opens you up from the inside. As it comes to its end it turns, becoming the letting go of the out-breath, a much different experience than an in-breath. Then comes a pause and another in-breath fills you up.

This circle of breath is the mother rhythm of Life and it has been with you since the moment you were born. As you ride the waves of your breath, open to the 'letting in' of the in-breath. If you watch carefully you will see how much you long to be opened up from the inside out through your breath. Then there is the wonderful relaxing and the 'letting go' of the out-breath.

To remind yourself that you are riding the waves of your breath say silently to yourself, "In…Out. Deep…Slow." Say "In" on the in-breath and "Out" on the out-breath. The same with "Deep…Slow." As you are learning to add these words to your breath, it can be helpful to write them on a card to have beside you. Leave space for two more pairs of words as we will add them in the coming chapters.

Every time you drift off into your thoughts again, no need to judge this. You have been paying attention to your thoughts for most of your life. Simply bring your attention back to being curious about the circle of your breath and these calming/focusing words. Stay with this as long as it interests you.

At the end, open your attention to include your whole body and notice what is different now that you have given yourself the healing of your own attention. When you are ready, open your eyes.

Abbreviated Version:

- Close your eyes and dip the finger of your attention into the river of your experience, noticing what it is like to be you right now.

- For at least three breaths, tighten your muscles on your in-breath. Then slowly, *very slowly*, relax everything on your out-breath as you say the great sound of letting go, "Ahh!"

- Now be curious about the circle of your breath as you say silently to yourself, "In…Out; Deep…Slow".

- Every time you drift off into your thoughts again, without judgment, bring your attention back to circle of your breath and the calming/focusing words. Stay with this as long as you are interested.

- At the end, expand your awareness and be curious about what is happening inside of you after a few minutes of conscious breathing.

- When you are ready, open your eyes.

Re-memberings

At the end of each chapter there will be a list of the main points of the chapter, along with enough space to write down what ideas touched you the most. This list will be helpful in keeping in the forefront of your awareness the shifts of perception that are happening for you as you go through this process.

- No matter what your mind says, everything is and always will be okay.

- You have a storyteller in your head that talks all day long and doesn't recognize this *okayness*.

- The storyteller tries to do Life rather than being open to it.

- Everything you long for and everything you truly are is always right here, right now.

- The doorway to freedom comes from your willingness to become curious about your own cloud bank of struggle.

- The more you bring the light of your compassionate attention to the stories you have been caught in, the more they thin just like clouds can thin when touched by the warmth of the sun.

- Life is completely different when you learn how to feel your way with your heart rather than thinking about it with your mind.

- Life is trustable. It is not always likable, but what's in the way IS the way.

- This trust is not trusting that you will get what you *want*. Trust understands that you will get what you *need* in order to come out of the cloud bank of struggle.

- The challenges of your life are for you. They are the yellow high-lighter of Life showing you the clouds of your reactive mind so that you can thin them with the sunlight of your own attention and thus rediscover the meadow of this moment.

CHAPTER 2

The Meadow of Your Being

When you are identified with the storyteller in your head which is the voice of your cloud bank of struggle, you live from a tight and small place – disconnected from your heart, disconnected from the amazing beauty and mystery of Life. To unhook from your storyteller is to become spacious and open – the opposite of the world of low-grade struggle that you are accustomed to. In unhooking, you discover how to use your mind for the exquisite tool it is rather than letting it be in charge. Let us take a few minutes to explore the amazing creativity of Life in order to get a feel for what it is like to unhook so that you can connect with the spaciousness and openness that is the meadow of your being.

Imagine living on Mars – red and rock. Now imagine being transported to the moon - brown dust and rock. Now see the Earth in your mind's eye and be stunned by how the creativity of Life was able to explode into a mind-boggling array of forms and colors - all the way from jungles filled with colorful parrots, to pristine icebergs floating majestically in silent waters, to miles and miles of coral beds that stun you with their beauty, to waves of grass dancing in the wind, to herds of baby seals with their liquid brown eyes.

This universe that you find yourself in has been unfolding for billions of years, birthing stars, exploding stars and then creating out of stardust this magical and mysterious planet we call home. If you start from the beginning and fast-forward, watching the unfolding of Life like a movie, you will see that forms continuously appear and disappear, whether it is a planet, a mountain, a ladybug or a human being.

In this process of appearing and disappearing, you have shown up. You have been given the gift of experiencing a tiny slice of this 14-billion-year process. What a valuable gift that is! It has been said that to be given a human Life is as rare as if there were just one golden hoop that floated on the seven seas of the world and just one turtle. Only once every hundred years does the turtle surface and it surfaces through the golden hoop!

For a moment allow your whole being to open into the joy of that. Life has been evolving for billions of years before you arrived and it will continue long after you depart, and for a few precious years you get to experience this constantly unfolding river of Life! The doorway back into consciously connecting with Life is this moment. This is the only moment that matters in your whole life. This moment where you are reading this book is the place where you can rediscover all of the joy, the creativity and the Love that is Life.

-Ω- Dip the finger of your attention into the river of your experience by lifting your eyes and simply open to your life as it is right now. See it. Hear it. Fully experience it. This moment is uniquely different from any other moment of your life!

Now realize that for most of your life you have missed it. You, like most people, withdrew from Life when you were very young, crawling into a conceptual world that keeps on churning out ideas about Life, but rarely, if ever, allowing itself to experience the real thing. Before you became immersed in a conceptual world, when you saw a cat, you really saw it; you really experienced the cat as a unique and amazing creation of Life. As you became entranced with the world of thought, you stopped fully experiencing Life. Instead, you experienced your ideas about it. As a Zen teacher once said, "No matter how many times you say the word water, it will never be wet." In other words, no matter how much you think about Life, it isn't the same as truly experiencing it!

So you walk around caught in your thoughts, homesick for a direct experience of Life. You long for it, but you are also afraid of it. You retreated into the world of your mind when you were young because life was big and unpredictable and scary. Your mind said, "Lets figure out how to control life and then we will be safe." So you have occupied your time trying to *do* life and *do it right*, not realizing that in the process, you turned into a *human doing* rather than a *human being*, trading the direct experience of Life for the illusion of control.

You stay caught in your mind, afraid of becoming fully who you are because you are not quite sure what that would look like. But I can assure you that seeing through your cloud bank and coming back to Life is the safest thing you will ever do for it is all about coming home! What that looks and feels like will become clearer as we explore the qualities of your essence and show you the skills that are needed to discover how to relate to your cloud bank rather than from it.

The Qualities of the Meadow:

On our adventure together we are exploring step-by-step how to see through the clouds of your mind so you can clear a pathway back into the meadow of your being. Before we start clearing your cloud bank, however, it is important to take a look at how you will experience Life living from the meadow. We need to do this because you were so conditioned to be afraid of Life when you were very young that if you don't recognize the safety and the joy of being open to Life, you will resist what is being offered here.

There are five core qualities that are the essence of the meadow of your being, and as you relearn how to open into Life, you will live from these qualities. They have always been with you, but you haven't noticed them because they have been covered over by the cloud bank of your struggling self. As we explore each of these qualities, I invite you to remember that they are with you right now as you are reading this book. Also, you don't need to find them. All you need to do is learn how to thin your cloud bank of struggle and there they are!

As we explore these five qualities, it is important to recognize that there is violence and chaos in the meadow just like in our lives. There are wild winter storms that rip branches off trees and wash away parts of the meadow. There is also death, for everything in the meadow appears for a time and then recedes back into mystery. The meadow includes violence, chaos and death but there is no resistance to them. These five qualities embrace the darker aspects of life rather than fighting with them. And if you look closely, you will see that new life is born from all of these.

The five qualities are:
- Flow
- Spaciousness
- Light
- Love
- Stillness/Peace

Flow:

Everywhere you look, Life flows. Rivers flow from the mountains to the sea; clouds flow across the sky; oceans flow in waves and tides. As air flows around this planet on the jet streams, wind dances through the trees and sap flows up from the ground. Blood flows throughout your body due to the pulsing of your heart at the same time information flows along your network of nerves.

In the great circle of Life, flow shows up in the dance of day and night and the changes from one season into the next. Death is also a part of this flow. Life arises out of mystery, expressing itself in an amazing variety of forms, and each and every one will dissolve back into mystery. Even the invisible world flows. Light shows up as waves of energy, each color being a different frequency. Sound is simply waves of vibration touching your eardrum.

Imagine the meadow 100 years ago and fast-forward the unfolding of this little piece of the planet. You will see that over and over again day flows into night and back again. Clouds come and go; sounds arise and pass away. Winter flows into spring; plants appear and dissolve away; animals are born and then they die. Everything in the meadow is about flow! Now expand your view and see this flow happening everywhere on our planet.

If you look closely, you will also see that there is an amazing Intelligence that permeates and penetrates the flow of Life. This Intelligence is so creative that you begin as just one cell, too small to see with the naked eye, then unfold into trillions of cells that all work together without a thought from you! When was the last time you worked to get your hair to grow or digest your food or beat your heart? This Intelligence is so smart that you can put two tiny seeds side-by-side and not see much difference in them. Then you plant them and one turns into a Sequoia tree and one a carrot. How does the seed know how to do that? The intelligent flow of Life!

The only thing in all of creation that doesn't flow is the cloud bank of the human ego. It has declared that there is a *me* in here and then there is Life *out there*. It believes itself to be separate from the flow of Life and believes that its job is to control it. It lives from fixed positions – good/

bad; right/wrong; liking/disliking. As long as you see yourself as separate, you will view Life as a potential threat and will withdraw from the flow of Life into the cloudbank of your mind.

All you have to do is look at the human condition to see how much suffering this creates. Most human beings live in a constant low-grade struggle inside of themselves. This struggle eventually shows up as all of the suffering on this planet – as greed, fear, hatred, despair, violence, loneliness. This belief in separation/control only gets stronger as we get older, cutting us off from the flow of Life. This separation from Life allows us to act in ways that hurt ourselves and others.

What would it be like to relax again into the flow of Life? Rather than trying to control Life, your intent is to open to its flow. You have known what it is like to be this intimately engaged with Life. Remember falling in love? There is lightness in your step, vibrancy in your being, and no need to have things be any different than what they are. Why do you feel this way? Because love has opened you again to Life. This is why most people are so addicted to love. It is one of the few experiences that can get through the cloud bank of struggle, inviting you simply to be fully here with Life. But as you have probably discovered, this kind of love doesn't last. Your cloud bank reconfigures and Life narrows down again to a chronic game of struggle.

It is possible to live from the ease that comes from discovering how to be open to the flow of Life. To open again, it is important to recognize that Life is an intelligent flow. You may not always understand or like it, but you can trust it. You can wake up every morning with a willingness to show up for the great adventure called Life. The key is to discover how to stay open to whatever Life is bringing you. As you do, you will come to the place where it doesn't matter whether you are falling in love, dying, feeling nauseated, anxious, witnessing a beautiful sunset, having a challenging conversation with your boss, or joyfully watching kittens. It is all just Life passing through the spaciousness of who you truly are.

To enter the flow of Life by being open to this moment – no matter what it is bringing you – is to learn how to fully feel, but not hold onto, wonderful states nor shut down and push the difficult ones away. Life will continue to give you both extremes of experience – joyful and sorrowful, easy and challenging, beautiful and unappealing. If your happiness is dependent on Life being a particular way, it is a given that the flow of Life will eventually dissolve the circumstances that are bringing you happiness just like the tide washes away your writing in the sand. And if you are afraid of the pains and discomforts of Life, you will resist them, turning them into suffering.

Joy, your natural state, isn't dependent on Life being any particular way. Joy comes from the ability to be fully engaged with the flow of Life exactly as it is appearing – no matter what it brings - allowing Life to pass through you rather than always trying to make it be a certain way. Peace comes when you discover that you don't have to tighten around the difficult nor hold on to the beautiful. As Pema Chödrön, an internationally known author and Buddhist nun says, "Peace isn't an experience free of challenges, free of rough and smooth; it's an experience that's expansive enough to include all that arises without feeling threatened."

-Ω- Take a moment and lift your eyes from the book and see with new eyes. Everything you see is Life flowing, and in that flow, everything in the space you are in has changed since you started reading. It may not look like that, but it is the truth. The sounds around you have changed; your body is a few minutes older; if you are inside, the rug and the lamps are a little bit closer to eventually going to the garbage dump; and if you are outside, everything in nature has altered with the flow of time. This all happens so slowly that we don't usually notice it, but it is happening none-the-less.

Spaciousness:

The second quality of Life that permeates the meadow of your being is spaciousness. If you look carefully, you will see that Life loves space. Right now, as you are reading this book, you are sitting on a planet that is dancing through vast oceans of space. For heaven's sake, it is 24,000,000,000,000 miles to the closest star. Then there are stars that are billions of times farther away than that! Can you even begin to imagine how much space that is? And this is all happening in a universe that seems to have no end.

Now let's go in the other direction – into your body. It is estimated that you are made up of anywhere from 70 to 100 trillion cells, and each of those is comprised of around 100 trillion atoms. If you blow up one of those atoms to be the size of a major league sports field, the nucleus would be a grain of sand in the middle of the field and the electrons would be dancing around the outside of the buildings. So even atoms are mainly made up of space, and because you are made up of atoms, you are space too! You probably experience yourself as solid, but science says that is just a trick of perception. Space is the truth of your being.

When lost in your cloud bank, you live in the tight and narrow space of your mind. When you are open to this moment, spaciousness permeates your body, mind and heart. Imagine a morning that you get up and the 'to-do' list is ignored. Instead, you luxuriate in bed. You linger at breakfast, and you follow your heart as to how the day will unfold. This is a day in which you feel the deliciousness of spaciousness. You unhook from the mental pressure of having to do something and instead enjoy Life. This is your natural state that can be accessed *no matter what is happening in your life*. To live from spaciousness doesn't mean that you will want to disengage from your life. It means that you won't be fighting with it anymore.

You can also unhook emotionally to give yourself the gift of space. Imagine a time when you have done something that you previously judged yourself for, and this time, instead of getting caught in self-judgment, you touch yourself with your own heart, accepting yourself as you are. This is giving you the space to be human, and it feels so much better than being lost in the tightness of self-judgment. Also, think of a time when your friend or mate acted in a way that upset you. Imagine instead that you decided not to take it personally and you let your reaction go. In both of these situations you probably took a deeper breath because you moved from the tightness of reaction to the openness of acceptance.

To experience how tight and small you usually are, think about being frustrated at the length of a stoplight. That may not seem like much tightness, but where is the joy? Then think of a time when you had a headache and you desperately wanted it to go away. Can you feel that in your resistance the tightness in your head gets stronger and affects, not only the headache, but your whole body?

Now let's go in the opposite direction. To get a sense of what spaciousness feels like, allow your imagination to recall a time where you were delightfully surprised by Life; or remember when a major project was completed and it felt like a huge weight was lifted off of your shoulders. Can you feel how your energy expands inside of you? When you are caught in the cloud bank of your mind, everything becomes contracted. The thicker the clouds, the smaller and tighter you become. When you stay open to Life, you are more spacious, so energy flows freely through you, allowing you to experience the pure joy of being alive.

Your birthright is to be the opposite of tight and small. Your natural state is openness, and it is only the cloud bank of your conditioning that causes you to tighten down and live small. It is possible to open again and live from spaciousness even if your mind is caught in judgment, your heart is sad, and your life is overwhelming. How can that be? Because your natural state is the meadow and from the meadow you can learn how to allow any reaction simply to pass through the spaciousness of your being.

-Ω- Take a moment and recognize that right now as you are sitting here, you are completely surrounded by stars. They are above you, below you, to the left and to the right of you. These stars are all dancing together and our beautiful planet is a part of this celestial dance. If your mind gets scared by the immensity of it all, hold its hand and invite it for just a few moments to become expansive and open. Stay with this feeling, allowing yourself to recognize how delicious it is to be this spacious.

Light:

As you reconnect with space and flow, you can know the third aspect of the meadow, light. In the Creation story at the very beginning of the Bible, it says, "And God said, let there be light!" And according to the Book of Genesis, this statement comes before the creation of the sun and stars. We think of light as coming from the sun, but the leading edge of science is now saying that *everything* is made out of light. David Bohm, the grandfather of quantum physics, once said that matter is just frozen light!

Arne Wyller, in his book *The Planetary Mind*, reports "Almost all of the particles in the universe are those of light." He goes on to say, "Light is a vital ingredient in all atoms." So it follows that since you are made out of atoms, you are made out of light! Most of the time, you dim the radiance of your being by only paying attention to the clouds of your mind, but it is possible to shine again like you did when you were young.

We have all met people whose eyes twinkle and whose presence radiates a sense of warmth. We oftentimes say they glow! That is what you begin to see when you rediscover the meadow of your being. Everything is made out of light whether it is a cat, a tree or even a rock! Everything shines from within, radiating the energy of its presence. You may not see this, but when you get quiet enough, you can feel it.

This is also true of all human beings, even though most of them have dimmed their light. The more you are lost in the problem factory of your mind, the thicker the cloud bank is around your head, cutting you off from the radiance of your body and the pure joy of being alive. No matter how thick your cloud bank becomes, however, it never stops the truth of your radiance.

Take a moment to shake one of your hands vigorously. Go for it. Now stop shaking, close your eyes and feel your hand. There is the flow of energy – the tingles, the aliveness. This is an artificial way to experience what it feels like when your energy is open and spacious. It feels good! It feels alive!

The ecstatic Persian poet Hafiz speaks directly to what we are talking about in his poem, *My Brilliant Image*:

> One day the sun admitted
> I am just a shadow.
> I wish I could show you
> The Infinite Incandescence
> That has cast my brilliant image!
> I wish I could show you
> When you are lonely or in darkness
> The Astonishing Light
> Of your own Being!

"The astonishing light of your own being' – what a wonderful phrase! You have so much energy within you that wants to be let out of the prison of your cloud bank of struggle so it can expand and dance, and when energy is free to flow, it shines. This is what you are hungry for – your own radiance. There is no accident that when a great burden has been lifted or you feel very happy, you oftentimes say "I feel so light!" It is also no coincidence that the word delight means 'of the light'! Even pictures of saints point to what we are talking about. The reason that most of them are painted with halos around their heads is because they broke free from the prison of the struggling self so their light could shine, and people recognized this light.

Plato once said, "We can easily forgive a child who is afraid of the dark; the real tragedy of Life is when men are afraid of the light." We are all afraid of our own light! You need to forgive yourself for being so afraid of opening to Life. You were scared out of it when you were very young. But even though you are afraid, you can learn the safety of opening again. You can, as Jesus invited us, learn how not to hide your light under the bushel of your cloud bank. This is the greatest gift you can give to humanity – to shine from within because you are open to Life. Carl Jung said, "As far as we can discern, the sole purpose of human existence is to kindle a light in the darkness of mere being." You too can shine and know the joy of your own radiance!

-Ω- Take a moment and shake your hand again. When you stop, bring the finger of your attention to your hand and feel the tingles. As they fade away, expand your attention and feel the subtle tingles all over your body that come from the energy of Life. If they are hard to find, put your attention a foot away from your body and then slowly bring it closer and notice the difference between the space around you and the actual experience of the energy of your body. That energy wants to expand and glow in joy!

Love:

When you rediscover the spaciousness of being open again to the great flow of Life, feeling energy moving through you rather than trying to control it, you begin to recognize that the word that best describes this movement of light is Love. There is great truth in the song title - *Love Makes the World Go 'Round.* It not only makes it go around, it is what permeates absolutely everything.

Eben Alexander, a neurosurgeon and author of the bestselling book, *Proof of Heaven*, wrote about what happened while he was in a seven-day coma from spinal meningitis. When asked what was the core of what he experienced while he was out of his body, he said, "Love is, without a doubt, the basis of everything... This is the reality of realities, the incomprehensibly glorious truth of truths that lives and breathes at the core of everything that exists or will ever exist, and no remotely accurate understanding of who and what we are can be achieved by anyone who does not know it, and embody it in all of their actions."

Physicist Brian Swimme calls this essence at the heart of Life 'allurement.' This force of attraction can be seen from the very beginning of our universe. The 'stuff' that arose out of the Big Bang followed the call of attraction and came together into communities we call atoms. The next step happened when these atoms were drawn together into communities called molecules. Then molecules were so attracted to one another they came together into communities called cells, and then cells followed the call of allurement and became multi-cell beings.

This attracting force at the heart of Life then showed up in the mating dance of insects and animals, and in their daily life, as well. In Charles Darwin's book, *The Descent of Man*, he mentions "survival of the fittest" only twice, but he mentions "love" 95 times when referring to the behavior of the creatures he was observing. He also talks about conciliation and cooperation being the most significant mode of behavior among them all.

This urge to connect at the heart of Life is all about Love. The great mystics of the world have all agreed that when you come out of the cloud bank of your mind, what you recognize and fully become is Love. And it is this Love, this allurement, this urge to connect, that brings all things together, whether it is subatomic particles or human beings or solar systems.

Every cell in your being is filled with this Love and it fuels almost everything you do; but you have been conditioned to search for it outside of yourself. This inevitably becomes the oftentimes endless, and mostly unsatisfying, search for somebody to love you. But what would happen if you recognized that the Love you long for is right here, right now? What would happen if you realized that Love is not something you need to find; it is who you already are?

Love is what constitutes absolutely everything. The more your heart opens, the more you can feel the energy of Love that animates everything - trees, rocks, birds, clouds, your dog and even the sun. Hafiz, who was truly awake to the Love at the heart of Life, speaks to this truth in his poem *The Sun Never Says:*

> Even after all these years,
>
> The Sun never says to the Earth "You owe me."
>
> Look what happens with a Love like that.
>
> It lights the whole sky.

Even the Sun is an expression of the Love at the heart of Life, endlessly giving forth its light! In its giving, the entire Earth thrives. In learning how to live from your heart, you become as lit up as the Sun, giving forth the warm, radiant energy of Love as you move through your day. Just as atoms, molecules and cells were drawn together into greater communities, you will draw others into the community of the heart. It is the heart that recognizes we are all unique expressions of the Love that is the essence of Life, and it is the heart that will wake us up to the truth that we are all in this together, floating on a tiny blue-green jewel of a planet that is dancing through vast oceans of space.

-Ω- Gently place your hand over your heart and contemplate the possibility that you are the lover you have been waiting for.

Stillness:

Look out at the world and see this dance of form that has been going on for eons – things arising and passing away - mosquitoes, dinosaurs, your great grandparents, mountains and even stars. Everything in this dance of Life appears and then eventually disappears. This constant movement of Life extends all the way out to the dance of galaxies and all the way within to electrons dancing around the nucleus of every single atom of your body. But that is only half of it. All of this movement arises out of a vast stillness, a stillness that births all the varied forms of Life.

Father Thomas Keating, a Trappist monk and one of the architects of Centering Prayer once said, "God's first language is silence. Everything else is a translation." If you find a quiet place to sit in nature and allow your mind to quiet down, you can feel the stillness and silence out of which all form arises and into which it returns in the ongoing cycles of birth and death.

This stillness is also within you. Eckhart Tolle, author of *The Power of Now* says, "Your innermost sense of self, of who you are, is inseparable from stillness." Yet most people know nothing of this stillness within. They have been conditioned not to listen. Instead they are so busy running here and there that it is almost impossible for them to simply become quiet, allowing their thoughts to settle, so that they can recognize this stillness and be nourished by its presence. It is possible, even in the midst of a busy life, to rest in stillness which opens you up to a deep and passionate listening to Life.

Even more than the joy of being open to the great flow of Life, you are homesick for this stillness. Because you were not trained to notice your own stillness, you can't tap into its wisdom. It is as if you have been at a beautiful outdoor symphony your whole Life and there has been one noisy person (your busy mind) that keeps distracting your attention from the symphony of your own stillness!

This stillness is not something you can search for. That is just more conflict – more trying to have your experience be different than what it is. The stillness at the core of your being is the absence of conflict, so trying to find it will only close the door to the stillness. In your willingness just to be curious about what is happening inside of you, the struggling self naturally calms down enough for stillness to reveal itself.

It is not an empty stillness you discover as you turn your attention within. It is full and rich, permeated with the Intelligence at the heart of Life. It is the source of "the still small voice" that is always with you. It is the place where you discover you are not alone. The presence of stillness, the knowing of stillness, the Love that is inherent in the stillness is always with you. When you recognize this, you are then able to partner with the wisdom of Life.

Being connected to stillness doesn't mean that you sit beside the road of Life, just resting in quiet and peace. In fact, the exact opposite is true. You become more fully engaged with Life, and your responses arise out of this stillness rather than coming from the busy mind that believes itself to be separate from Life.

> -Ω- For a few moments, close your eyes, and watch how busy your mind is. Know that underneath all of that noise is a field of deep stillness. This stillness is always with you, and you can discover how to rest in its embrace.

As you drink in these five qualities that are at the core of who you truly are, it is important to recognize that they are here with you right now! You may not notice them, but they are always with you no matter what is happening in your life. As you see through your cloud bank, you begin not only to recognize these qualities, but also live from them, and this brings you to the *okayness* we explored in the last chapter.

The cloud bank of your mind is dualistic in nature, so on some level it is always setting up what it likes against what it doesn't like, which is the game of not okay! The meadow is beyond this dualistic game of struggle. The meadow includes rather than excludes; it allows rather than resists; it accepts rather than rejects, all bringing you to the *okayness* that comes from showing up for Life!

The rest of the book is about accessing these five qualities that make up the meadow of your being. You won't be reconnecting with them by trying to find them. That just creates more struggle. Instead, you will learn how to see through the cloud bank of your mind so it can thin and you can discover the joy of living from these five qualities of the meadow rather than from your mind that is usually busy doing Life.

RE-MEMBERING SECTION

This week's Re-membering Statement:

The meadow is here right now

or

_____ is here right now

(Name one: flow, spaciousness, light, love, stillness)

Your Own Statement:

_____

Re-membering Session

This week we are exploring a powerful way to calm down your cloud bank of struggle so it will become easier to reconnect with the five qualities of the meadow. This will be done by the simple act of deepening your breath through focusing on the out-breath. If you are timing your session, add one minute, taking it to six minutes. If time is not an issue, stay with each step as long as your curiosity is engaged.

Let's begin:

- Close your eyes and dip the finger of your attention into the river of your experience, noticing what it is like to be you right now.

- For at least three breaths, tighten your muscles on your in-breath and then very slowly relax everything on your out-breath as you say the great sound of letting go, "Ahh!"

- Bring your attention to the circle of your breath.

  Deepen your out-breath by imagining a lit candle floating in the air in front of you. Breathe in through your nostrils and then gently blow out through your mouth, imagining you are blowing out this candle. As you become comfortable with this rhythm, allow yourself to enjoy the deliciousness of a long, slow out-breath.

As you become comfortable with a longer out-breath, you can let go of the candle image and breathe in and out through your nostrils, enjoying a long, slow out-breath. Say silently to yourself, "In...Out; Deep...Slow". Stay with this as long as it interests you.

Whenever you notice that you are no longer paying attention to the circle of your breath, no judgment. Simply bring your attention back.

- For a few moments at the end, open your attention to include your whole body and notice what is different now that you have given yourself the healing of your own attention.

- When you are ready, open your eyes.

Abbreviated Version:

- Close your eyes and dip the finger of your attention into the river of your experience, noticing what it is like to be you right now.

- For at least three in-breaths, tighten your muscles and then *very slowly* relax everything on your out-breath as you say the great sound of letting go, "Ahh!"

- Bring your attention to the circle of your breath.

- Imagining there is a lit candle in front of you, breathe in through your nostrils and then blow out the candle, enjoying a long, slow out-breath.

- When you are ready, let go of the candle breath and breathe in and out through your nostrils, as you say to yourself, "In...Out; Deep...Slow".

- When you notice that you are no longer paying attention to your breath, simply bring your attention back with no judgment.

- For a few moments at the end, open your attention to include your whole body and notice what is different now that you have given yourself the healing of your own attention.

- When you are ready, open your eyes.

Re-memberings

- When you live in the cloud bank of your mind, you live tight and small – disconnected from your heart, disconnected from the amazing beauty and mystery of Life.

- Life has been evolving for billions of years before you arrived and it will continue long after you depart, and for a few precious years you get to experience this constantly unfolding river of Life!

- The five qualities that are the essence of the meadow of your being - flow, spaciousness, light, Love and stillness - have always been with you, but you haven't noticed them because they have been covered over by the cloud bank of your struggling self.

- As your cloud bank clears, you begin not only to recognize the five qualities but also to live from them, and this brings you to the *okayness* that is your natural state.

- To enter the flow of Life by being open to this moment – no matter what it is bringing you – is to learn how not to hold onto wonderful states nor push the difficult ones away.

- To come out of your cloud bank is to become spacious and open – the opposite of the world of low-grade struggle that you are used to.

- You have so much energy within you that wants to be let out of the prison of struggle so it can expand and dance and shine. This is what you are hungry for – your own radiance.

- The Love you long for is right here, right now. It is who you really are.

- All of Life arises out of a vast stillness and this stillness is the essence of who you really are. It is full and rich, permeated with the Intelligence at the heart of Life.

- You can't try to find the five qualities. That just creates more struggle. Instead you can get to know your clouds so they can thin and the five qualities will reveal themselves.

CHAPTER 3:

Fear – It's Nothing to Be Afraid of

Picture the meadow in your imagination and recognize that the flow, the spaciousness, the light, the Love and the stillness that permeate the meadow are inside of you right now. These five qualities make up your natural state, and there is a deep longing in you to know and live from them. Now see yourself standing in the meadow. You always are in the meadow but you don't recognize it because your head is surrounded and filled by the cloud bank of struggle you were conditioned into when you were young. Now see the clouds dissipating and feel yourself fully present with the light, love and stillness of the meadow. Experience the joy of that!

The way you come back to the meadow is by getting to know your storyteller which is the voice of your cloud bank. So the next step on our journey together is to show you how to become curious about what stories you are running in your head rather than being lost in them. I invite you to imagine while you read this chapter that you are sitting in a movie theater, watching your life on the big screen. A unique feature of this movie screen is that you can hear the storyteller in your head!

It's amazing when you realize that most of the time you aren't aware of what your storyteller is saying. Rather than being curious about what stories are going on in your head, you just tumble from one thought to another all day long. The doorway to freedom comes when you can see what your mind is doing rather than being identified with its stories.

As you hear the stories in your mind emerging on the screen, the first thing you are bound to notice is how much your mind struggles. It struggles with big things and little things. It is often upset about aspects of your body all the way from the shape of your nose to a life threatening disease. And it is very used to being frustrated by what other people are doing, ranging from how they are driving to your difficult boss.

If you watch the screen closely, though, you will see that it isn't always struggling. If your mind gets what it wants, it can feel quite good. You have the new iPad and it is great fun; or your favorite contestant on the reality show is ahead of everybody else; or somebody you like a lot says "I love you." But up on the screen you can see clearly how this kind of happiness is only there as long as things are going the way the mind wants them to go. If the iPad gets stolen, or you don't have enough money to buy the upgraded version, or the contestant is voted off the show, or your partner's behavior upsets you, the storyteller in your mind gets upset and starts to struggle with what is, and the scenes on the movie screen turn into struggle again!

Watching carefully you will see that the storyteller inside of your head swings from liking to disliking all day long. It likes the weather or it doesn't. It likes its mate or is frustrated with him/her. It likes the chocolate cookies, only to eat too many, and then it doesn't like itself. It likes when your life is very busy and is scared when not enough is going on, or vice versa. It likes when the stoplight is long enough to put on your makeup. It dislikes the length of the stoplight when you may be late to work. Once you see this pendulum inside of you that swings between liking and disliking all day long, you recognize how exhausting this is!

What if on the armrest of your theater seat there were a bunch of buttons that allowed you to change not only what you were thinking and feeling but also other people's behavior? This is one of the favorite strategies of the mind. It says that if you could just change your mate or your boss or your friends or your child, making them be the way you think they should be, then everything would be okay (or would it?)!

You also do this same thing with yourself. It is very seductive to feel that if you just made yourself different, then you would finally know the peace that you are searching for. Up there on the screen you can watch yourself doing affirmations, or promising you will never be compulsive again or trying to think positive thoughts, but you can also see that these may help only for a period of time and then the struggling self takes over again. So back to the buttons you go, becoming frustrated and despairing that you haven't been able to get yourself together. No wonder most people don't live from pure joy!

-Ω- Step out of the movie theater of your mind and dip the finger of your attention into the river of your experience, keeping your attention fluid and open. You may notice the sounds around you, or a slight headache, or a feeling of peace, or a tickle on your back, or a mind that is resistant to doing this. Simply notice what you notice when you turn your attention to Life. Little moments like this matter. Just as drops of water created the oceans, moments of being fully open to Life help to thin your cloud bank so you can rediscover the meadow that is always with you right here, right now.

Your Childhood and Fear:

An interesting question to ask is, "What fuels the struggles of the storyteller in our heads?" There is one simple word that sums it all up – fear. Most people, most of the time, are caught in a low-grade fear that at times can flare into anxiousness, insecurity, and even full-blown terror. Let us now look at fear so you can get to know it because in this knowing lies the possibility of not being controlled by it.

It is true that fear is a part of Life. Think about stepping off the curb and hearing the sound of a truck barreling down on you. Without a thought, you leap back in fear. That kind of fear is necessary for survival, but it is only about 1% of the fear you experience. Most of what you experience is psychological fear. It is the stories of fear that move through your mind all the time.

Sometimes there are big fears like the fear of illness and death. Sometimes they are smaller like, "Will my pants fit?" Whether fear shows up as the slow drip of insecurity or it comes to visit you in the middle of the night, shaking you to your core, fear is always narrating your world. You are so enamored by fear's need to make sure the next thing goes right that you can't really enjoy Life!

It wasn't always that way. When you were very young, you knew instinctual fear - you startled at the sound of a loud noise or were overwhelmed by things you experienced when your parents left you alone. But these clouds of fear would pass through you, leaving hardly a trace. It didn't take long before you began to know psychological fear. When you were small, the world was big and scary. Everybody around you was like a giant - you barely came up to their knees. These big and sometimes scary giants had crawled into their cloud banks a long time ago and they often acted in ways that were confusing and frightening.

Some of us had parents with cloud banks full of lightning and thunder. Most of us had parents whose cloud banks were just foggy. They had left themselves for the world of their minds when they were growing up and, living in their cloud banks, they didn't know how to fully connect with their children.

Also, in their disconnection, all parents give their children two core wounds – invasion and abandonment. Being invaded can range from having a parent that constantly denies your feelings, to sexual abuse. Abandonment can vary from an overly busy parent that doesn't have time for the child, to one that actually walks out and never comes back. So whether your parents were stormy or just foggy, mildly abusive or majorly, this generated fear inside of you as you tried to make sense of what was going on.

-Ω- Notice what is happening with your breath right now. Are you holding it because of what we are exploring? If so, blow out the candle for a few breaths before you continue reading.

Your Mind-Made-Me:

Because our parents had left themselves for the world of their minds, most of us, when we were young, didn't have people who could truly listen and help us with all of the overwhelming thoughts and feelings we were experiencing. So you, like most children, began to tell yourself stories about what was going on in order to try to manage your fear. This was the creation of the storyteller inside of your head, or what Eckhart Tolle calls "the mind-made-me." This is the place where the wispy clouds that formerly passed through the meadow of your being begin to circle around your head, cutting you off from your heart and ensnaring you in the world of your mind.

To call it a "mind-made-me" is a very powerful way to describe what most people experience as themselves. The *me* you think you are is just a collection of thoughts, feelings and beliefs that is based on fear. Your *mind-made-me* is the storyteller that tries to manage Life so, hopefully, you won't get lost in the fear inside of you that you are so afraid of. I also like *mind-made-me* because it alludes to the possibility of another sense of you. Not another *me*, so to speak, but another place to live from – the meadow.

The creation of this storyteller in your head didn't happen overnight. Slowly, almost like putting together a 10,000 piece picture puzzle, you organized your experiences into a self-image that allowed you to feel the illusion of having some control over this huge thing called Life. The key here is the word 'image.' It means "a likeness or representation of something." The storyteller is not the real thing – it is ideas about Life and it becomes the cloud bank that cuts you off from the living experience of Life.

As you are watching your storyteller up on the movie screen, you can see that at one moment it thinks of you as a good and together person and then, in a flash, if somebody judges you or rejects you, that image can change into unworthiness, insecurity, anger or self-judgment. That is how ephemeral your self-image is.

> -Ω- Now push one of those buttons on your arm rest that takes the movie back to a day in your childhood before you were six. Remember, you can hear what is going on in your mind up on the screen. Allow yourself to view an experience with your parents that scared you. Know you had many moments such as this as you were growing up, and as you listen to what is going on inside of you, you can watch your storyteller being developed. Allow your heart to open to how scary life was at times and how alone you oftentimes felt.

Your Child-Made Me:

As we explore this storyteller inside of you, at times I will call it the "child-made me," for it is important to realize that the self-image you function from as an adult was created in your mind when you were a child. Psychologists say that your view of yourself and of Life was pretty well formed by the time you were six years old. So the beliefs, attitudes, wants and fears that move through your head all day long (and cut you off from fully experiencing Life) were created in the mind of a child!

-Ω- Take a moment and let that in. If you are honest with yourself you will see that most of the time you are pushed, pulled, prodded and engulfed by thoughts and feelings that have been with you since you were very young – the longing to be liked, to be perfect, to be the best, to be safe, to be in control, to be right; the belief that you are less than, not enough, the sense that if only you were able to change yourself and your life, then everything would be okay. The stories that these beliefs spin in your mind may change over the years, but the essence of them is the same as when you were young. So if you look very closely at what goes through your mind all day long, you will see that the self-image you crawled into as a child is still alive and active inside of you!

If you could go back and be inside of yourself when you were two or three years old, you would be able to recognize the growing insecurity in your mind – the fear of your parents leaving, the devastation of being teased by an older child, the jealousy of having your sibling get the bigger popsicle, the grief when a beloved toy is lost.

Then if you were able to visit yourself when you first went to school, you would see how overwhelming it was. We all had moments when we were growing up where we felt vulnerable and exposed. People said mean things to you, they used you, they judged you, they teased you, and they rejected you. Out of this arose the fears that you were not doing it right, were not good enough, or would be rejected. These fears followed you throughout your schooling, along with the deep fear that sometimes threatened to overwhelm you when you were all alone – the fear that you wouldn't be able to keep everything together.

Then there was adolescence. The desire to fit in was one of the core things that ran you and, like most kids, you did some crazy things in order to belong. You may have starved yourself or scarred your face from trying to get rid of your pimples or you became caught up in putting other people down in order to feel more powerful. The sad thing is that most children, even the children in the in-crowd, believe that they are not enough.

> -Ω- Go back to the theater again and push the button that will take the movie back to your adolescence. Allow a challenging experience from that time to show up on the screen. Can you allow this awkward, easily confused and quickly embarrassed adolescent into your heart?

The Continuation of Childhood Fear:

The fears of our childhood don't go away. In fact, they get buried inside and then influence us from underneath our everyday awareness. Let's imagine as you watch yourself up there on the movie screen that you are attending a party, and let's listen to what may be going on inside of your head: "I talk too much." "I don't talk enough." "Another drink will make me feel better." "She is prettier than I am." "I think I am doing this pretty well" "He could never be interested in me." "All I want to do is get out of here." "I don't know what to say." "What happens if there is a lull in the conversation?" "I am not smart enough to contribute to what she is saying." "I should have….I shouldn't have." "They don't like me." "I should be more outgoing." "I want another drink." "I was the life of the party." Even believing that you *did the party right* comes from fear that you could have *done it wrong*.

Then imagine what happens that night after the party, when you are awakened by a racing mind that critiques everything you said and did at the party with a sinking sense that it wasn't okay. What doesn't show up on your screen is that the other people at the party are unconsciously run by these deep fears too, and may very well be critiquing how they did. Fear is so embedded in us and our fear of looking at it is so great that one of the core functions of our storyteller is to keep us as far away from our fear as possible!

The fear-based mind doesn't only talk loudly about parties. There are all sorts of life experiences that bring it to the forefront of your mind. There may be an important business meeting the next day or a trip to a new destination or a visit with a challenging relative or a doctor's visit about the lump in your breast. It also shows up in the everydayness of Life – "I am going to be late." "I am not dressed right." "I followed the wrong directions." Whether it is everyday fears or the big ones, most people, most of the time, have some level of fear moving through their minds.

-**Ω**- Settle into the theater again in your imagination (maybe even smell the popcorn!) Push the button that will take the movie to an embarrassing experience you had as an adult. Allow yourself to re-experience it as fully as you can up there on the screen. Recognize the voices of fear and self-judgment that arose inside of you. Know that these voices can be set free so that you can simply be yourself with no fear or self-judgment talking away in your head.

The Price of Fear:

Most people are not aware of how afraid they are of Life. Rather than trusting Life, the storyteller inside of them believes that it has to *do* Life and *do it right*, while secretly believing that whatever it does is not enough. Your storyteller longs to be loved, but doesn't know how to love itself. It wants desperately to be understood by others, but does not know how to be with itself in an understanding way. It is afraid of rejection and thus is usually concerned about what other people think of it. It oftentimes feels unworthy and becomes very busy trying to hide the so-called unacceptable parts of itself from the world. It feels a lot of guilt about the most inconsequential things (although it doesn't believe they are inconsequential!). And this guilt fuels shame, the sense that there is something bad and wrong about itself.

Because of this chronic sense of struggle in your head, the storyteller is constantly chasing happiness, believing that it will be happy when it *does life right* and thus gets everything *together*. But for everybody, this getting it all together comes and goes in a flash, and when it slips away, the storyteller is off again on the pursuit of happiness, trying to get what it wants and get rid of what it doesn't like. Can you feel how frustrating that is? Can you feel how heart-numbing that is?

You pay a heavy price for living from your fear-based storyteller and then spending your life trying to outrun it. For this moment, can you notice the storyteller inside of you that has been trying its whole life to keep everything together and the fear that generates this? Can you see that to be run by this struggling storyteller makes it impossible to experience Life simply and clearly?

As you were growing up, the more you were engulfed by the world of fear, the thicker your cloud bank became. In that world of fear, something even more debilitating happened – you became afraid of your own fear. So your life became a game of trying to feel good in order to leave fear behind. But this never lasted because it was based on fear! And the more you got caught in the world of fear, the more you lost sight of the meadow of Life.

When your endless trying doesn't bring the results you want (because you can never know the lasting happiness you long for within the cloud bank of the mind), the storyteller then gets lost in its stories of shame, anger or despair, which are also based in fear. Shame is the fear that you are not doing your life right; anger is the fear that you are not getting what you want or you are getting what you don't want; and the fear that despair is built upon is the feeling that you never have or never will get what you want.

The shame, anger and despair of your storyteller feed one another. Anger can go all the way from subtle irritation to white, hot anger - anger at Life, anger at people that are not *doing it right* and anger at itself for doing the same. The storyteller then oftentimes gets caught in self-pity, feeling like a victim and thus feeding despair which can go from a little melancholy to full blown depression. In this victimhood, the storyteller either blames others for its suffering, e.g. "If only he would….." or "Why did she?" or it blames itself which feeds the shame.

We have all experienced this vicious circle of shame, anger and despair that can arise from the depths, taking over our lives. This despair that is at the core of this circle has some very dark fear-based stories - "This is all there is." "It will never get better." "There is no way out of this darkness and I am here because I have done 'it' wrong." Most people are so afraid of this despair that, rather than meeting it within themselves, and thus freeing it up, they spend their lives trying to run away from it.

But remember, as you are watching the movie screen and listening to the conversations inside of you head, you have never left the meadow of your being. You mostly don't notice it because you have been so trained to listen only to your storyteller. In order to unhook from its stories it is important to look this deeply and clearly into its world.

> -Ω- Lift your attention from the book and notice something outside of your storyteller like the dance of shadow and light in the area around you or the sounds of Life as they appear and disappear. Know that the amazing unfolding of Life is always happening right outside of the world of your storyteller.

Our Shared Experience:

Isn't this amazing that all of this is happening inside of you, underneath your everyday awareness? This isn't just you. Most everybody has these ongoing conversations inside because they are identified with their own storytellers that are based on fear! I know it may not seem that way because most people are very good at putting on a mask, hiding their fear from themselves and from others. It is no accident that the root word for personality is 'persona,' which means 'mask.' So don't be fooled by appearances, for they can be deceiving.

A friend once told me about a woman she worked with whom she truly admired (and felt envious of), for this woman had the fancy car, designer clothes and the high powered job that we think of as the trappings of success. One morning this seemingly together person asked my friend to come into her office where she revealed she had tried to kill herself the night before because her life had no meaning. So know you are not alone in having a storyteller that is based on fear and glued together with judgment – no matter what it looks like.

> -Ω- Back in the movie theater, push the button that projects on the screen somebody you think has it all together like a motivational speaker or a famous doctor. You can hear the voices in their heads just as you could yours, and as you begin to hear their inner voices, recognize that they carry many of the same fears and judgments that you do. They may not fall into them as much as you do, but they have a storyteller too!

The reason we may not be fully aware that this is all happening inside of us is because we have all been conditioned to run away from fear as fast as we can. This is why we are such a compulsive society. We are so deeply afraid of our fear and the anger and the despair it generates that we create elaborate systems for not seeing them. In order not to experience what we are experiencing, we turn to food, drugs, alcohol, busyness, to-do lists, the internet, television, shopping, etc., to keep ourselves numb. We even use meditation to get to the states we want and to get rid of the ones we don't. We distract ourselves with a fervor that is astonishing! The sad thing is that even though distraction may bring us temporary relief, it does not heal this underlying movement of fear.

Getting to Know Fear:

-Ω- Take a moment to dip the finger of your attention into the river of your experience. See it, hear it. Fully experience it. This moment is different than any other moment of your life. In this moment of purely noticing Life, there is no fear.

You just lifted your attention out of the fear-based mind and used it to notice Life. Of course, the mind may have resisted doing this or, after a moment or two of pure connection, it pulled your attention right back into the world of time, for fear needs time to exist. It needs stories of past and future in order to get a foothold in your mind. But every moment when you have let go of relating to life through fear and instead opened to Life truly makes a difference – even if it happens for just one second.

What counts even more is being able to see the fear that clouds your direct experience of Life. In order to see fear more clearly, it is helpful to recognize that fear also affects your body as well as your mind. Watch yourself the next time you are suddenly startled or somebody judges you, and you will see your body tightening. Because fear causes you to tighten it shows up as tension headaches, trouble with your jaw, frozen shoulders, difficulty breathing, stiff necks, stomach problems, back aches, etc. Many of your physical difficulties and illnesses are fueled by the contraction of fear because it constricts the healthy flow and functioning of your body. You are also conditioned to try to get away from your fear by numbing yourself through compulsions, and most of them wreak havoc in your body.

When you live in the fear-based stories of your cloud bank, you *react to* Life. When you live from the meadow of your being, you *respond to* Life. In the meadow you relax; you are open and available to Life. When identified with stories of fear, you get tight, resisting, reacting and manipulating. Take a moment and be honest with yourself as to how much you live in reaction. Many times you react to little things your friends and loved ones say, creating drama in your world, drama that is all based on fear. Remember that commercial about the wife asking the husband about whether her jeans make her look fat? Her fear is that he will say she looks fat and he fears not saying it right! That is how so many people live their relationships. Fear not only prevents an authentic and truly intimate relationship with yourself, but also with others.

At the core, fear causes you to contract rather than open, to protect rather than connect, to resist rather than respond, to survive rather than thrive. Fear constantly makes demands, and you have spent your life trying to meet them. You don't have to live your life with fear in charge. Can you feel the relief of that? It is possible to come out of the trance of fear and live from the aliveness, openness and joy of the meadow.

-Ω- Take a moment and dip the finger of your attention into the river of sensations that is your body. Are you holding tension in one shoulder (or maybe both!)? Or are the muscles right above your pubic bone being tightly held? Or is your brow furrowed or possibly your jaw clenched. Whatever you notice, for this moment, invite it to let go.

The Way Out:

The way out of the trance of fear is to get to know it, for whatever your mind does to attempt to get rid of fear causes more fear. It is possible to become honest enough with yourself to be able to start looking at what goes on inside of you, and in that looking, you become free. For as soon as you can see the stories of fear you crawled into, you can begin to see *through* them and come back to the meadow of Life. The renowned writer and speaker Krishnamurti once said:

> It is not that you must be free from fear. The moment you try to free yourself from fear, you create resistance against fear. Resistance in any form does not end fear. What is needed, rather than running away or controlling or suppressing or any other resistance, is understanding fear; that means watch it, learn about it, come directly into contact with it. We are to learn about fear, not how to escape from it, not how to resist it.

In order not to be controlled by fear and to do what he is suggesting – to look at your fear – it is important to ask, "Do I want to be free from fear?" Initially there will probably be a response of, "Yes, I do." But that will probably be followed by a response such as, "It is scary to look at my fears," and that is just fear, afraid of looking at itself! But when you really look at your fear, you will see that it is made up of stories that were conditioned into you when you were young and they are nothing to be afraid of. It is just fear! I assure you, looking at fear is one of the safest things you will ever do once you learn the skills of how to see fear rather than believing its stories.

Pema Chödrön tells about a repetitive dream she had when she was younger. In the dream, a monster was chasing her and she always woke up in terror at the place where the monster was about to get her. When she told a friend about the dream, her friend suggested that Pema turn around and look at the monster. That thought so frightened her that in subsequent dreams she kept on running. Then one night as she was again running away from the monster, a wall appeared in front of her blocking her escape. With great trepidation, she turned to look at the monster and to her surprise, the monster stopped and didn't come any closer. She then noticed that the monster had pink fingernails! In that moment she woke up, and she never had that dream again.

This dream represents the power of turning and looking at fear itself rather than letting it influence you from underneath your everyday awareness. At first it is scary, but slowly you realize how scared your storyteller is and you begin to see that it has been for a very long time. Your heart, however, is not afraid. It is your heart that can bring your fears the attention they need in order to be healed. That is why the monster had pink fingernails. How could you be scared of a monster like that?

I was raised in an environment that fostered terror, and I became so caught in the world of fear that in my early twenties I tried to kill myself three times because the intensity of the fear that I lived in was unbearable. My fear showed up as dread – the combination of feeling something really bad is going to happen and the belief that it is happening because I have done something very wrong. I tried psychiatrists, psychologists, group therapy, counselors, medications, affirmations, hospitals, meditation, hypnotherapy, and anything else I could find in order to try to outrun my fears.

It was only when I was taught how to turn toward my fear, becoming compassionately curious about its story rather than trying to fix it or get rid of it, that the pressure began to be released. Fear will always be a part of me, but whereas it used to be 110% of me, now it is only 5%, and when it does arise, I can listen to it rather than getting lost in its story. In that listening, it calms down through the healing energy of my heart.

-Ω- What would it be like to get to know your fears rather than being afraid of them? Live in that question, rather than thinking you have to do anything about it.

Fear and the Heart:

A few months ago I read the novel *Magic Hour* by Kristin Hannah that reminded me how deeply our fears long to be touched by the acceptance of our hearts. This novel is all about the antidote of meeting fear right where it is. It is the story of a little girl who at around the age of four was kidnapped and bound in a cave in the forest for a couple of years. She eventually got free after her captor hadn't come back for a long time, and she showed up in a small town close to the forest. She had lived without loving human contact for so long that she was like a wild child. She didn't speak, she ran on all fours and she howled.

In the story, a very aware child psychiatrist begins to work with her, and what happens between the adult and the little one speaks directly to what will heal the fear inside of you. When I finished reading the book, I did something I have never done before with a novel, I immediately read it again, for it touched me deeply to watch this little girl come back to Life.

To me, the little girl was an extreme representation of the scared one inside all of us, and the psychiatrist was the antidote. She gave the little girl what she most needed - loving presence. Rather than trying to fix or judge her, she met her right where she was, and in that accepting attention, the little girl starts to slowly open to people. You watch how the strength of fear inside of her wars with the longing to trust the loving presence of the psychiatrist. As the little girl comes out of her shell, you get to hear how fear operates inside of her and how it is fueled through shame. You also get to see that it is the heart that heals.

You are the loving presence that your fears have been waiting for your whole life. It is your heart that will heal them, and it will also heal all of the stories in your head that your fear generates. For the rest of this book we will explore how your fear can heal through the power of your accepting attention. Learning how to look and listen to the stories of fear that have been driving you your whole life, will free you from their grip.

-Ω- Are you breathing shallowly? Allow a deep breath and recognize for a moment that your fear is afraid and needs the acceptance of your heart in order to let go.

No Need to be Afraid of Fear:

As you come close to your deep fears in order to give them the attention they need to let go, you will have moments where you will feel the fear of taking one more step closer to your fear. But remember, fear is nothing to be afraid of. It is just a story in your head and 99% of your fears have never come true. Samuel Clemens, whose pen name was Mark Twain, once said, "I have been through some terrible things in my life, some of which actually happened."

It is helpful to remember that fear closes you down, keeping you caught in the game of resisting Life, which builds a wall between you and Life. This wall of resistance stops Life from flowing through you, cutting you off from the joy of being fully alive. Would you rather keep fear locked up inside of you where it can tell you all sorts of stories that generate everything from unsettledness to full-blown terror? Or would you rather come back to the meadow of Life by getting to know the fear-based storyteller in your head?

You don't need to be afraid of looking at fear. In order to discover the courage to look at your fears, it is important to know that even when you are caught in fear, it is happening within a greater space in you that is not afraid. This meadow of your being has ALWAYS been with you - even right now as you are reading this book – and it is absolutely okay with whatever is happening.

It is also important to know that our fear doesn't want us to be afraid of it. Instead, it wants to be seen, to be welcomed, to be touched by our hearts so it doesn't have to be afraid anymore. Or as Austrian poet and novelist Rainer Maria Rilke says in *Letters to a Young Poet*, "Perhaps everything that frightens us is, in its deepest essence, something helpless that wants our love."

You can discover how to bring this sense of being okay to your fear. In fact, your fears have been waiting for you to be present with them your whole life! As you give fear the space to be, it then can pass through you, opening you again to the meadow of your being.

-Ω- Check in to your body again and see if the place that you invited to let go a few pages back is holding again. Understand that it is fear that causes your body to contract. Open to one deep breath and invite this area to let go. Even if it tightens again, this moment of letting go matters.

RE-MEMBERING SECTION

This week's Re-membering Statement:

This is only fear

Your Own Statement:

_____

Re-membering Session

We have explored this week that fear comes from your storyteller and that you have been deeply conditioned to fear Life. But we also recognized that fear is always happening within the greater space of the meadow of your being. To turn on the calming aspect of your nervous system so that the cloud bank of fear can thin, we will add another pair of words to the "In...Out, Deep...Slow" you have been saying to yourself as you ride the waves of your breath.

The words are 'calm' on the in-breath and 'ease' on the out-breath. Allow yourself to feel these words rather than thinking about them. You are not trying to calm yourself. You are simply inviting calm and ease through feeling the essence of these words. If you have written the first two pairs of words on a card, add these now. Also, if these words resonate with you, you can also use them any time to focus and calm your mind.

If you are timing your session, add one minute taking it to seven minutes. If time is not an issue, stay with each step as long as your curiosity is engaged.

Let's begin:

- Close your eyes and dip the finger of your attention into the river of your experience, noticing what it is like to be you right now.

- For at least three breaths, tighten your muscles and then very slowly relax everything on your out-breath as you say the great sound of letting go, "Ahh!"

- Bring your attention to your breath and relax into its nourishing circle, feeling the opening of the in-breath and the letting go of the out-breath.

Remind yourself that, for these few minutes, you are inviting your mind to rest on your breath, by saying silently to yourself:

In...Out, Deep...Slow, Calm...Ease *

When your attention goes back to the thoughts in your head, do not judge how much this happens but be willing to bring it back to the circle of your breath and the calming/focusing words.

- For a few moments at the end, open your attention to include your whole body and notice what is different now that you have given yourself the healing of your own attention.

- When you are ready, open your eyes.

These words are a part of a meditation that Thich Naht Hahn, the beloved Buddhist monk and author, taught to the children of his community. They are so powerful in calming and focusing the mind that when the adults heard about them, they started using them too!

Abbreviated Version:

- Close your eyes and dip the finger of your attention into the river of your experience, noticing what it is like to be you right now.

- For at least three in-breaths, tighten your muscles and then very slowly relax everything on your out-breath as you say the great sound of letting go, "Ahh!"

- Bring your attention to the circle of breath, saying the calming/focusing words silently to yourself.

- When you notice that you are no longer paying attention to your breath, simply bring your attention back with no judgment.

- At the end, expand your awareness and notice what is different after a few minutes of conscious breathing.

- When you are ready, open your eyes.

Re-memberings

- Most people, most of the time, are caught in a low-grade fear that at times can flare into anxiousness, uncertainty, and even full-blown fear.

- Whether fear shows up as the slow drip of insecurity or it comes to visit you in the middle of the night, shaking you to your core, fear is usually narrating your experience.

- This storyteller in your head is not the real thing – it is just a collection of thoughts, feelings and beliefs that were created in your mind as a child, and they are based on fear.

- The fears of our childhood don't go away. They get buried inside and then influence us from underneath our everyday awareness.

- We are so afraid of our fear and the shame, anger and despair that it generates that we create systems for not seeing it – like compulsions, busyness, and endlessly trying to fix.

- You pay a heavy price for crawling into the cloud bank of fear and then spending your life trying to outrun it. You don't have to live your life with fear in charge.

- To try to get rid of fear causes more fear. The way out is to get to know fear.

- Do I want to keep on running away from fear my whole life?

- The more you look and listen, the more your heart opens to how scared your storyteller is.

- You are the loving presence that your fears have been waiting for. It is your heart that will heal them, along with the other stories that fear generates.

- As you allow fear the space to be, it can then pass through you, opening you again to the meadow of Life.

- So don't be afraid of looking at your fears. Fear is always happening within a greater space in you that is not afraid.

CHAPTER 4

You Are Not Alone

Now that we have seen that the foundation of the storyteller that fills up your head is fear, and we've come to know the world of fear a little better, it is time to learn the art of turning toward your experience rather than being lost in it. The first and most important step is to recognize you are not alone. There is an Intelligence that is with you every step of the way. If 'Intelligence' isn't the right word for you, you may resonate with 'Presence,' or 'Guides,' or 'God,' or 'Beloved' or 'Wisdom Self,' or 'Angels,' etc. All allude to the same truth: that you are not walking the path of life alone – you just think you are. So even though you may not recognize it, there is support that has always been with you and always will be. "Recognize" is the appropriate word, as what we are exploring here is a re-knowing of this most basic truth of Life.

Oprah, in her farewell show, spoke directly to this. She used the word 'God,' but I like what Stephen Levine says, "I can use the word 'God' because I don't have a clue about what that means, but there is nowhere I see it not." Oprah said,

> I have felt the Presence of God my whole Life, even when I didn't have a name for it. I could feel the voice bigger than myself speaking to me, and all of us have that same voice. Be still and know it. It's always there speaking to you and waiting for you to hear it. In every move, every decision, I wait and I listen. I am still. I wait and listen for the guidance that is greater than my meager mind. So what I know is God is Love and God is Life, and your life is always speaking to you.

Most of us, however, feel alone with no sense of inner support as we make our way down the path of our lives. But even though we may feel alone, we aren't. There truly is a Presence bigger than us that is speaking to us all of the time. To discover this truth is like two fish that jumped out of the water at the same time, and one said to the other, "Now I know what they mean by water!" The fish were so immersed in water their whole lives that they didn't recognize it. We are so immersed in our storytellers that we don't see that loving support has always been with us.

The Spells:

Let us now look at what keeps us separate from the support that is always with us. Come back to the meadow metaphor. The cloud bank of struggle that surrounds your head keeps you cut off from the meadow of your being and the truth that you are not alone. It is made up of core beliefs you took on when you were very young, and these beliefs are the foundation of your storyteller. These beliefs are so deeply embedded in most of us that we usually are not aware of them. I like to call these core beliefs 'spells' because they are concepts that were superimposed on you, they are not true, and they can be lifted.

Rather than buying into the spells, you can learn how to see them and recognize how they generate habitual patterns of thinking that keep you lost in the cloud bank of your storyteller. To see them more clearly, it helps to understand that there are eight core spells we all take on. They can be divided into three types of spells. The first two are what I call 'Foundational Spells.' Then come the three 'Operational Spells' that describe how we function after having taken on the first two spells. Finally, there are the three 'Hidden Spells,' which describe the core wounds we all carry from having identified with the spells. Here is a list of the eight spells, broken down into the three categories:

- **Foundational:** "I am separate from Life," and thus "Life is not safe."

- **Operational:** "I must control Life, "I must do it right," and "I am not doing it right enough."

- **Hidden:** (Because I am not doing it right) "I am wrong," (thus) "I am unlovable," and this leads to the core spell, "I am all alone."

Let us explore each one of the spells. (See Appendix 1 for a list of the eight spells.)

The Two Foundational Spells:

Somewhere in the first year of your life, as thoughts began to drift through your head, you took on the **first Foundational Spell**, which is "I am separate from Life." In other words, you think there is a 'me' inside of you who exists separate from Life, which is 'out there.' That is like one cell in your heart saying, "I am separate from the heart and my life has nothing to do with all of the other cells that make up the heart, let alone the rest of the body!"

This spell of separation is truly insane, and it is the opposite of what is true. To be able to see this spell, I often have people in my retreats spend time with a piece of food, like a strawberry. I begin by telling them they are not holding a strawberry. They are holding the whole universe, because it took everything throughout all time and space in order for this strawberry to exist.

What we now know is that every atom that makes up a strawberry was once a part of a star, for stars were the incubators for most of the elements of Life. So this strawberry needed stars in order to exist. It also needed the creation of the Earth and all of the creativity that has happened for the past 4 ½ billion years. This brought forth the mother plant of this strawberry which came from a seed, which came from another seed and so on down through the corridors of time. Where does that continuum end? It is a thread of Life that goes all the way back to the beginning of our universe.

The strawberry would not exist without the sun that gives of itself day in and day out. It also needed water, which is a very rare occurrence, at least in the parts of our galaxy that we have been able to explore. How could that water continue to circulate and give birth to Life without the atmosphere and the winds that make up what we call "weather"? This strawberry also needed mountains and trees that dissolved into soil, along with the bacteria and the worms in the soil that made it alive. It even needed the blue green algae that oxygenated our planet many billions of years ago making cellular life possible.

-Ω- Look up from reading this book and recognize that everything you see is made out of atoms that were once a part of a star!

So this one little strawberry needed the sun, the stars and all of the creativity that has happened on this planet in order to live. It is dependent on most everything for its existence. The same is true for you! It is purely an illusion that you are a separate being. Just as that cell in your heart is not separate from the other cells in the heart and your heart is not separate from the whole of your body, you are not separate from the whole of Life.

You are intimately and intricately connected with absolutely everything throughout all time and space. Would you exist without the sun, stars, water, Earth and sky? No! Would your life be able to continue without bees to pollinate your food, migrant workers who harvest it, people who drive the trucks to the market, the people who drill for the oil that allows the trucks to run? We could go on forever. You are dependent on everything for your existence and thus you are connected with everything.

Einstein spoke to this when he said:

> Many times a day I realize how much my own outer and inner life is built upon the labors of my fellow men, both living and dead, and how earnestly I must exert myself in order to give in return as much as I have received.

He was talking about the people who make his life possible. We are talking about *all* of the creativity of Life that is necessary for you to exist.

It is not only on the physical level that separation is an illusion. The interconnectedness of everything happens on all levels of existence. Take a look around the space you are sitting in and notice that it really seems that Life is just a collection of separate objects, including you. But science is now revealing to us that everything you can see is an outer expression of a field of energy, and this field connects it all at a very deep level.

It may help to imagine that Life is like a tree. This tree has roots you cannot see and it is because of those roots that the trunk, the branches, the leaves, the flowers and the fruit can show up. Life is like that. Everything you see arises from the root of Life which is a field of energy, and in that field, everything is connected everywhere at all times.

This means that every atom, molecule, rock, bug, person, planet, bacteria, star, and blade of grass is a unique expression of this underlying energetic field, and this includes you. You are a necessary expression of the same unified field. Just like a cell in your heart could be said to be a separate cell, but it is also part of a greater whole called your heart, you are a necessary and unique expression of the greater whole called Life.

What we are exploring here is in contradiction to the concepts of Newtonian physics that we were raised in, the kind of physics that says that everything is separate. We're finally waking up out of that dream. Physics is now helping us to see what the great mystics have known forever – that Life is like a spider web. One tiny movement on the web is felt by the whole web. Lift your hand and wave it in the air. On some very deep level, the plants, people and animals around you felt your movement. You are a part of this web and your movements move the web.

So everything – absolutely everything – arises out of this web of being, is intimately connected to it, is animated by it and then will eventually dissolve back into the field just like a wave in the ocean arises and then recedes back into the ocean. The wave is not separate from the ocean; it is the ocean temporarily expressing itself as a wave. The same is true for the people and things in your life. So in a very real sense, there is only one of us here! We are all just an outer expression of an inter-connected web of being in which everything is dependent upon everything else for its existence.

-Ω- Lift your eyes from the book and take a moment to recognize that everything around you is just the outer expression of an inner world of energy.

It is hard for us to imagine that nothing is separate, that everything arises out of one interconnected web of being. So take a moment to realize that we have bought into some pretty big illusions in the past. Think of the belief that the world was flat. People of that time laughed at the scientists who were saying the Earth was round. They said that was ridiculous and could easily be proven false, for if it was round, everybody would fall off of its surface!

The spell that we are separate from Life is a big illusion human beings became caught in that appears to be true, but isn't. As we have been exploring, it does help to begin to see that on the physical and energetic levels nothing is separate. But it can also help to recognize how much suffering is caused by buying into this spell. Because we are unaware that we are one family, it lets us buy into the belief that we are different from one another. So most of humanity is caught in the adolescent belief that my skin color, my politics, my beliefs, my sexuality, my opinions, my gender, my religion are better than someone else's.

This spell creates boundaries that separate us whether it is in our intimate relationships, our politics or our religions. The belief in separation even goes so far as to create artificial things called national boundaries, and then we fight over those boundaries. Feeling we are separate from the Earth has also allowed us to plunder and pollute her everywhere. Ultimately this spell detaches you from the unfolding of Life causing you to lose trust in Life and in yourself. This cuts you off from the pure joy of being alive. Seeing how far from the truth this spell is would be very funny if it didn't generate so much suffering.

The **second Foundational Spell,** "Life is not safe," comes out of the first spell, and it is one of the deepest illusions human beings take on. Life is a highly intelligent, benevolent, unfolding force that includes violence and death, *Life is for Life* and it knows what it is doing. Yes, there is pain in Life, but there is much more suffering when you aren't open to its flow. It is not always likable, but it is always *for* you. This is the spell of fear that we explored in depth in the last chapter.

-Ω- Take a moment to dip the finger of your attention into the river of your experience. Be curious about what it is like to be you right now. Know this moment in your life is unique. When you are fully present with this moment, you have stepped outside of your spells.

The Three Operating Spells:

This belief that Life is something to be afraid of then brings forth the **first Operating Spell**: "I must control Life." This spell is like one cell in your heart deciding it has to beat and regulate the heart! This spell is so strong in the human mind at this stage of evolution that most people don't have a clue that what is in charge of Life is the Intelligence that has been orchestrating the dance of Life for billions of years and that regulates their hormones and beats their hearts.

This spell of control generates the **other two Operating Spells**, "I must *do it* right" and "I am not *doing it* right enough." This is the vicious circle most people live in most of the time – they try to *do* Life and *do it right*, all the while secretly believing they are not doing it right enough. This circles them back to the belief that they must do a better job of controlling themselves and Life. True healing never happens through the struggle inherent in these three spells. It happens when you can see them and unhook from their stories. That is why the peace and joy you long for don't come from changing anything! They come from the ability to see and unhook from your spells.

At first, it is a foreign concept that you don't need to spend your time manipulating your experience of life. It is foreign because you and everybody else have been conditioned to believe that your job is to make your life be what you think it should be. In other words, you've been trying to create a particular reality rather than showing up for reality!

As it begins to dawn on you that trying to control Life cuts you off from fully experiencing Life and that maybe Life knows what it is doing, you begin to recognize the truth that it is safe to open to its creative, intelligent flow. Yes, that flow includes pain, loss and death. We have tried to control Life in order to get away from these seemingly unlikable experiences. But the suffering we create for ourselves by resisting Life's flow is far greater than the pain we experience by being open to all of it.

This can be very scary at the beginning, for being lost in the illusion of control is like walking down the path of Life enclosed in a suit of armor. As you begin to relax into Life, the pieces of the armor start falling away and you feel unprotected and naked. In order to discover the courage it takes to step out of the illusion of control, feel what would be more alive – clanking down the path of Life in a suit of armor or stepping out of its prison and freely walking, skipping and dancing down the path?

It is courageous to contemplate the possibility that Life wouldn't fall apart or explode in your face if you didn't spend your energy trying to control it. But the more you awaken, the less interested you are in controlling Life and the more interested you are in connecting with it – opening to its creative flow, which includes both the dark and the light of Life. In that opening you discover that the safest and the most creative thing you can do is to loosen your grip on control.

> -Ω- Let go of reading and bring your attention to the circle of your breath. As it settles there, say silently to yourself: In...Out; Deep...Slow; Calm...Ease. Give yourself this gift for a few minutes, and when you are ready, resume reading.

The Three Hidden Spells:

The longer you live from these operational spells, the more they bring you to the **three Hidden Spells** we all have: **I am wrong** (because I am not doing Life right), thus **I am unlovable**, and that means **I am all alone.** These are the secret fears that reside within all human beings and are so deeply embedded that most people are not even aware of them (most of the time!) and when they are, they definitely don't want anybody to know they feel this way.

The "I am wrong" spell is the world of shame. Every human being carries some level of self-judgment. It is called guilt and it can be a useful tool for maneuvering through Life. But within most human beings this voice has grown to enormous proportions, moving from the level of "I've done something wrong" to "I am wrong." Usually subtly, but sometimes quite loudly, it compares you to some mythical idea of who you should be and then berates you for coming up short of perfection.

Have you ever been afraid to tell a loved one the truth about a part of yourself because you were scared they wouldn't like you? That is the "I am wrong" spell that says, "I am not good enough, right enough, perfect enough to be loved." If you doubt you have this inside of you, imagine that there is a machine that can read your thoughts and then announce them over a loud speaker – all of them! You, like most people, probably had a moment of cringing when you imagined your most secret thoughts being made public. If you look closely at what you don't want others to know about you, you will see at the core the belief, "Because of these thoughts and actions, I am bad and wrong!" This spell can become so strong inside of you that it completely blocks out your beauty, uniqueness and perfection, freezing you out of Life.

The more you buy into the spell of "I am wrong" the more it opens you into the second hidden spell of "I am unlovable." The reason why this spell is so devastating is because you need connection in order to survive. When you were very young you were extremely vulnerable. Everything was much bigger than you were and definitely more powerful, and the primal need for survival was coded in your genes. There was a part of you that knew that these giants you lived with (called parents) were the ones who could either give or withhold the essentials — food, water and shelter.

Deep inside, you understood that to please them brought forth connection; to not please them meant pain. So you learned very early on to try to be the right kind of child. Ram Dass, author of *Remember, Be Here Now*, calls it 'somebody training'—learning the skills to be what you *should* be according to your family system and your society.

You not only put all of this energy into becoming what you thought you had to be to get your needs met. You also did this to get their attention, because attention is necessary for survival. In the 1950s, Dr. Harry Harlow of the University of Wisconsin took a group of baby monkeys from their mothers at birth. They were put in cages all by themselves and then given a choice of two surrogate mothers. The first was a wire monkey that could feed them from a bottle suspended at its center. The second was a cloth monkey that, while it did not feed them, could be held close for comfort. Whichever one they chose, they were cut off from the other. Over and over the baby monkeys chose the comforting cloth monkey over the wire monkey that could feed them. The nourishment of comfort was more important than the nourishment of food![1]

The more you feel lovable, the more connected you become with yourself and with life. The more the "I am wrong" spell takes over, throwing you into the belief that you are unlovable, the more disconnected you become, and this opens you to the last of the Hidden Spells, - "I am all alone." This is the deepest fear inside of most human beings. In fact, when we lived in small tribes, the fear of banishment was more powerful that the fear of physical punishment.

The amazing thing is that the feeling of being alone is the opposite of what is actually happening. This is what we are exploring in this chapter. You have not been, nor ever will be, alone. There is Presence within you that is with you, supporting you and loving you every step of the way.

-Ω- For a few precious moments, let go of everything except a full recognition that this is the only moment that matters in your life. The more your attention and your immediate experience come together, the more you will discover you are not alone.

All of these spells are created out of fear and held together with judgment and they cause you to buy into the belief that you are all alone.

You discover the untruths of these spells (and thus unhook from your storyteller so you can recognize the meadow of your being) by experiencing what you are actually experiencing with curiosity and compassion.

When you can stand with a particular spell, it opens the door into the contrasting experience. In my life, as I was able to be with my extreme self-judgment, that tightly held energy opened up into compassion. As I was able to be with my deep fear, giving it the accepting attention it needed in order to let go, my fear became a doorway into joy and a deep trust of Life. Or, as a friend once said, "Fear is just exuberance without a breath!" And, as I was able to be with my despair, I discovered that I am not alone.

To get to know the world of spells further, there is an appendix at the end of the book that lists the eight core spells. Listed under each spell are a variety of different ways that your storyteller may speak them. It can be very helpful to read this list and check off the stories that you recognize. It will allow you to get to know your storyteller more intimately.

-Ω- Pause for a moment and take a breath. Now breathe out one long, slow out-breath and contemplate the possibility that you can discover how to see through your spells and live from the meadow of your being.

What is God?

In order to discover that you are not alone, it is important to explore the whole concept of God. Down through history, human beings have lived with some inkling that there is something bigger than us in charge, and we, in the Judeo-Christian culture, have called it God (Dieu, Dios, Dio, Die, Gott, Adana, etc.). We first saw it as supernatural beings that had to be placated by sacrifices and doing everything 'by the book.' We then matured into the idea that God is a man (with a beard) sitting in heaven, deciding whether we were good enough to enter. Gradually, instead of seeing God as a personification of a human being, more and more people began seeing God as a supernatural being. Some see God as a heavy taskmaster and some as more benevolent, but this supernatural being is still seen as something outside of them.

We are now ready to take another step in our evolution of understanding what God is. And that is: God is a verb! It is not a being or thing that can be defined, rather it is *Being* expressing in and through and as everything, including you. God is the unified field that permeates and animates all of Life. What is called God is the *Intelligence* at the heart of Life. This takes it out of the ideology and rules of religion and makes it available in the immediacy of our lives.

So how do you know that this Intelligence is and always has been with you as Oprah Winfrey declared? If you just take a moment to reflect, you will see that this is true. For heaven's sake, at one moment you were just one cell that was so tiny it couldn't be seen with the naked eye, and it eventually multiplied into trillions of cells. As this multiplying happened, each of those cells knew which system they were to be a part of (like the circulatory system or the nervous system) and they knew exactly what their tasks were within that system. Now all of those trillions of cells digest your food, repair your cuts, beat your heart and regulate your PH without a thought from you. In other words, you are a walking, talking sea of Intelligence!

> -Ω- Pause for a moment, close your eyes and open to the intricacies of this Intelligence at work in your body right now! Put your finger on your neck and feel the flow of blood pulsing throughout your body. Recognize the amazing creativity of all of your white blood cells that are protecting and healing. Now put your hand on your chest and acknowledge all of the work of the little alveolus in your lungs that allow oxygen into the blood stream and absorb toxins into the lungs so they can be breathed out. All of this is the working of this vast Intelligence at the heart of Life.

The Intelligence that is running your physical body is just one facet of the vast Intelligence that is in charge of Life. It also permeates and penetrates all levels of your existence, including your mind and heart. The best word I have ever come across to describe it is Presence. This Presence is always with you. You already have a relationship with it; you just may not notice it. It is always speaking to you, but you oftentimes don't hear it because the voice of your storyteller is so loud.

Asking for Help:

There is a powerful story that Martha Beck, a long time columnist for *O Magazine*, wrote in her book called *Expecting Adam*. It speaks directly to the truth that we are not alone and help is always here. This book is about her pregnancy with her second child, Adam, who has Down's syndrome. At the time she became pregnant, she had been at Harvard for many years, doing her undergraduate, graduate and post-graduate degrees. Harvard revered the mind as the place to go for answers to Life's questions and so did Martha. But Adam changed all that. She says, "By the time he was born, she unlearned virtually everything Harvard taught [her] about what is precious and what is garbage!"

During the pregnancy, Martha was working on her post-graduate degree, parenting her two year-old daughter, and oftentimes functioning as a single parent when her husband went on trips to Asia for his graduate work. As soon as she became pregnant with Adam, she started having experiences that could only be described as out-of-the-box of 'normal'. One of the most powerful experiences happened in the fifth month of her pregnancy. Sleeping with her little girl while her husband was away, she woke up in the middle of the night to a wet bed. She checked Katie's diaper only to find it dry. When she went to the bathroom and turned on the light, she discovered herself covered in blood. (Later it was described as a placental obtrusion.)

She was so light-headed by the loss of blood that when she called the University Health Services (no 911 in those days) and described her symptoms, they told her she had to get to the emergency room right away. She was so weak that she was unable to tell them that her husband was gone and she didn't have the support she needed to get there. After she hung up the phone, she started drifting in and out of consciousness, and as her normal perceptions faded, she felt presences in the room. She could not physically see them or hear them, but she could feel them and she said, "Their presence was as real and ordinary to me as the presence of oxygen." She says that she doesn't know what these presences were. The normal terms such as angel, ghost or sprit didn't work for her. She finally decided that the best word to describe them was 'friend.'

As she grew weaker, she asked for help for her baby. She was very cold due to the loss of blood, and immediately on asking for help she started to become warm and the bleeding stopped. She said it was extremely soothing but then their support left and she became cold again and dizzy from the loss of blood. She said she then did one of the hardest things she has ever done, and that was to ask for help for herself. Immediately she felt a set of hands holding her, a wonderful warmth emanating from them. This calmed her deep fear, replacing it with a knowing that both she and her baby were out of danger. She then said, "I did not fall into sleep that night. I rose into it out of the black, cold pool as though I were being lifted by a thousand wings." She was never quite sure what happened that night, but as her life force was fading away, she accepted things that she would have disbelieved at any normal moment.

What did make sense to her was that as she asked for help, she opened what she calls "a cosmic door" an inch or two. She could see that this kind of help had always been there for her, she just didn't know it. It also made sense that the reason why she hadn't been aware that support is always available was she didn't know she had to ask and that asking opens a door!

The Power of Questions:

How do you ask for help? How do you discover that 'friends' are always with you? First, by understanding that you have been conditioned to believe in the **two Foundational Spells** of: "I am separate from Life" and "Life is not safe". These brought you to the **three Operating Spells**: "I must do Life", "I must do it right", and "I am not doing it right enough". And the **three Hidden Spells** of "I am wrong", "I am unlovable" and "I am all alone," tighten the noose of separation, cutting you off from the help that is always there. Remember, when Martha asked for help for herself she said it was the hardest thing she had ever done!

As long as you buy into the illusion that you are separate from Life and, because you fear it, you must be in control, you will be cut off from the vast *Intelligence* within you. Be patient with this. You and most everybody else have been caught in these spells for most of your life. But you have now drawn into your life the shift of perception that will allow you to unhook from them, and in that unhooking, discover that you are not alone.

The most skillful way I have discovered to be in relationship with Presence is to ask questions without looking for an answer. This may seem strange at first because you are so used to asking questions and then trying to figure out the answer. But that approach asks your mind for the answers and your mind is mostly lost in the cloud bank of your conditioning, cut off from the wisdom at the heart of Life.

Looking for answers in your mind oftentimes leads to tension and frustration. The mind works well for objective questions that have definitive answers, but have you ever closely watched yourself when you were trying to figure out the answer to a subjective question such as "Should we get married or not?", "Should I buy this car or not?" One moment getting married or buying that car seems like a good idea and the next moment it doesn't. That is what it is like to use your mind for the answers to many of the questions in your life.

Instead, you can go directly to the *Intelligence* at the heart of Life. To ask a question and then let it go is one of the most powerful tools a person can learn on this journey back to him or herself. The power of a question isn't in the answer; it is *in the question itself!* In some very deep and profound way, the answer isn't important. What is important is to become a question. Why is this so powerful? When you ask a question without looking for the answer, you are circumventing your mind, creating a space inside of you where the *Intelligence* of Life can be heard. It is guaranteed that Life will fill that space with the answer at the right time, for the energy of Life always fills a void.

You have experienced the truth of this many times in your life. A simple example is trying to remember another person's name. You go to your mind and you can feel the name is "right on the tip of your tongue," but you are frustrated because you can't seem to get to it. You then go on with whatever you are doing and awhile later the name pops into your mind! That is the mechanism we are talking about here. As soon as you let go of trying to find the name, the question you asked, "What is his name?" begins to work its magic from underneath your everyday awareness and up pops the name. The key is not to look for an answer. This can be challenging at first for you are addicted to answers. Answers give you the illusion of control, but being the space of a question allows you to live the answer, becoming a partner with Life.

-Ω- Dip the finger of your attention into the river of sensations that is your body. Are any of your favorite places of tension holding on? If so, choose one area and tighten it on your in-breath and then, very slowly, let it go on your out-breath.

I was reading a novel by Jacqueline Winspear the other day and there was a passage that poetically describes what we are exploring here:

> Truth walks toward us on the paths of our questions. As soon as you think you have the answer, you have closed the path and may miss vital new information. Wait awhile in the stillness and do not rush to conclusions no matter how uncomfortable the unknowing. Stay with the question.

Take a moment and let that in – "Truth walks toward us on the paths of our questions". In other words, you create an opening where truth can speak to you when you ask a question without looking for an answer. It doesn't have to be uncomfortable. Many times it won't be. You just ask a question and let it go, knowing the answer will appear in the right time and the right way.

Being given the gift of accessing the power of asking questions without looking for an answer is like being given a sacred talisman from Life that is there for you no matter what is happening. You may not notice how powerful this is at first, so just keep on asking. In the beginning, the mind won't have a clue about the phenomenal power of asking questions without looking for an answer. It will still look for an answer. It will also doubt that anything will happen and it will forget to ask. That's just what minds do. But keep on asking and the fogginess of your mind that can't hear the answer will slowly lift and you will live the answer!

Some of my favorite questions are: "What am I ready to see here?" "What is the way through this?" "What do I need to say/do/be that is for the highest good?" "How can I serve?" "What am I?" "What is asking for my attention?" If these don't call to you, ask Life, "What are my questions?"

Most of us will experience the answers to our questions through a simple knowing, more like an Aha. You know what I mean - that moment when something clicks inside of you and it is very clear that it is the truth. It may come to you in the shower, or reading a sentence from a novel, or something that is said in a movie. However it comes, the more you ask questions, the easier it becomes to feel the answer.

Also know that these answers won't necessarily come in your desired time frame. You signal Life with a question that you're ready to live the answer, and then Life lives it through you at the appropriate time. Where I am in the process is that most answers easily and quickly appear within me, but there are questions I have lived in for years and I am still growing into the answer. I know that the answers will come at the right time.

-Ω- Take a moment and ask Life to show you your spells. Then let that question go so it can work its magic from underneath your everyday awareness.

Through asking questions without looking for an answer, have a conscious conversation with Being itself and discover you are not alone. Take the courageous step of knowing that Life is smarter than you and that it knows what it is doing with you. Turn the challenges of your life over to Life, over to that which is bigger than you and has been orchestrating the dance of Life for billions of years. Then be willing to listen, for Life is talking to you all of the time.

Finally, be willing to relax into the process. The answers to your questions will be lived through you in Life's time and in Life's way. Your questions will help to dissolve the cloud bank of your spells, revealing to you the meadow of well-being that is always with you, the well-being that knows that no matter what is happening in your life, it is all okay.

RE-MEMBERING SECTION

This week's Re-membering Statement:

I am not alone

Your Own Statement:

_____

Re-membering Session

In order to see more clearly all of the spells which keep you cut off from the support that is always with you, it is helpful to discover how to see what your storyteller is doing when your attention drifts back into the world of thought. You do this by noticing whether it is telling itself stories about the past or the future.

Read through these instructions then put the book down and begin exploring. If timing your session, add one minute, taking it to eight minutes. If time is not an issue, stay with each step as long as your curiosity is engaged.

Let's begin:

- Close your eyes and dip the finger of your attention into the river of your experience, noticing what it is like to be you right now.

- For at least three in-breaths, tighten your muscles and then _very slowly_ relax everything on your out-breath as you say the great sound of letting go, "Ahh!"

- Bring your attention to the circle of your breath, saying the calming/focusing words, "In...Out; Deep...Slow; Calm...Ease."

As you ride the circle of your breath, whenever you find yourself paying attention to your storyteller again, notice if you are telling yourself stories about the past or the future. If your stories are about the past say, "Past", then bring your attention back to the circle of your breath. If you notice your thoughts are about the future, say "Future" and then return to your breath. If you can't immediately see past or future or you are just spacing out say, "Story." Then return to the circle of your breath.

- For a few moments at the end, open your attention to include your whole body and notice what is different now that you have given yourself the healing of your own attention.

- When you are ready, open your eyes.

Abbreviated Version:

- Close your eyes and dip the finger of your attention into the river of your experience, noticing what it is like to be you right now.

- For at least three in-breaths, tighten your muscles and then *very slowly* relax everything on your out-breath as you say the great sound of letting go, "Ahh!"

- Bring your attention to the circle of your breath, saying the calming/focusing words.

- When you find yourself paying attention to your thoughts again, notice if you are telling yourself stories about the past or the future and name what you notice. If you are not sure, say "Story".

- Then bring your attention back to the circle of breath and the calming/focusing words.

- Expand your awareness and notice what's different about your experience after a few minutes of being with yourself.

- When you are ready, open your eyes.

Re-memberings

- The cloud bank of struggle that surrounds your head is made up of core beliefs you took on when you were very young. We are calling them 'spells' because they are concepts that were superimposed on you; they are not true, and they can be lifted.

- Spells keep you cut off from the support that it always with you.

- You are not walking the path of Life alone – you just think you are.

- Believing that you are separate from Life has cut you off from a conscious conversation with the Intelligence of Life.

- Everything you can see is an outer expression of a unified field of energy in which everything is dependent upon everything else for its existence.

- Life knows what it is doing and it is safe to open to its flow.

- Trying to control Life cuts you off from fully experiencing Life.

- God is a verb! God is not a being or thing that can be defined, rather it is *Being* expressing in and through and as everything, including you.

- Presence is always with you, you just don't notice it. It is always speaking to you, but you don't hear it because of the noise of your storyteller.

- To ask a question and then let it go is one of the most powerful tools a person can learn for the power of a question isn't in the answer - it is *in the question itself!*

- The key is not to look for an answer. In the beginning, the mind will look for answers, doubt anything may happen, and forget to ask.

- Take the courageous step of trusting that Life is smarter than you and it knows what it is doing.

- Turn the challenges of your life over to Life – over to that which is bigger than you and has been orchestrating the dance of Life for billions of years. Then be willing to listen, for Life is talking to you all of the time.

CHAPTER 5

The Healing Power of Curiosity

Once you begin to

- see that most of the time you pay attention to the storyteller in your head that is based on fear and glued together with judgment,

- see that these stories were created in your mind when you were young, and they struggle with Life, usually wanting things to be different than what they are.

- contemplate at least the possibility that you are not walking this path of Life alone, that there is a field of wisdom inside of you that is always there and that you can turn to for help,

then the next step is to discover how to see your clouds and see through them so that you can recognize the meadow of this moment, rediscovering how to relax into its flow. For remember, you have never left the meadow, you just think you have. And to try to fix, change, get rid of or rise above your stories is just more struggle.

To connect with Life – to know again the joy of being fully alive - you need to see what is within you that blocks you from full connection with Life. You need to get to know your cloud bank of struggle, the spells (beliefs) it is made up of and the stories that are present when you are caught in a spell. This ability to see the spells that make up your cloud bank without identifying with their stories comes from the ability to look – to be with what you are actually experiencing with curiosity and spaciousness.

The best way I can describe this is through what I call the One Thousand Doors metaphor. Imagine being imprisoned in a room where every wall is filled with doors and each one promises a way out of the prison. This room represents the cloud bank of your struggling self. Some doors promise that if you fix your "problems" then everything will be okay. Others promise that if you just ignore them, understand them, deny them, try to numb out or run away from them, you will be out of the prison. So you try 999 of the doors many times and one of three things happens: The door is locked; the door opens to a brick wall; or the door opens and you walk through it, only to find yourself in the same room.

There is one door you have never tried. It is a very small door in the bottom of a dark corner and you can see there is a word written on the front of it, but you can't quite tell what it says. The first two letters are 'He' so you figure that is the doorway to hell and you stay as far away from that door as you can!

But there comes a time, after you have tried each of the 999 doors many times with no lasting results, that you figure Hell has to be better than this. So you go over to the corner, crouch down in front of this little door, and much to your amazement, you see the word that is written on the front of the door is 'HERE.' You realize in a flash that this door is an invitation to be curious about your experience rather than always trying to make it be different than what it is. But this door looks too small to get through and so your mind doubts that simple curiosity will be able to help you out of this prison.

However, since everything else failed, you decide to give it a try. As you cultivate curiosity, an amazing thing begins to happen. The more you are curious, the more the door expands. And without even noticing it, rather than walking through the door and out of the prison of your mind, the walls of the room slowly dissolve and you find yourself fully connected to Life again!

The Art of Looking:

-Ω- Stop reading for a few minutes and place your attention on the sounds around you. Notice that they are different than the previous times we have tuned into listening. Notice how they appear and disappear. Every single sound is brand new, even if you think you have heard it before. You are listening to the sound track of your life, and as you stay with it, you will see that sounds arise and pass away. Be curious. There are loud sounds and soft sounds; sounds close to you and far away; even sounds inside of you. Stay with this as long as it interests you, and when you are ready, come back to the book.

In these few moments, you were curious about Life rather than thinking about it. Curiosity is the ability to bring your attention and your immediate experience together. As your attention becomes engaged with what is happening right now, you will discover that there is a whole lot going on around you that you never notice. It is Life, and when you are curious you make a direct contact with it, experiencing it the moment it appears out of mystery.

We have all had moments when we are fully here for Life, but it is so easy to drift back into our stories about it. Hopefully you have now discovered that there is a big difference between your stories about Life and Life itself. It is also important to know that your storyteller is afraid of being this open to Life. It wants to pull your attention back into the web of stories in your mind. This is where the power of curiosity can begin to transform your cloud bank of struggle so you are again available to Life.

To discover the art of being curious about what is going on inside of you so your cloud bank can thin, you first need to know that Life's pure energy is continuously pouring through you. And as it flows through your mind and body, it gets condensed into ripples of thought, sensations and feelings. But these are not who you truly are. You are awareness. You are that which can watch thoughts, feelings and sensations pass through the vast spaciousness of who you really are.

To get a sense of this, close your eyes and silently say the word 'peace' a number of times. If you watch carefully, you will observe that there is a part of you saying it and there is part of you that is aware that it is being said. This awareness is who you really are. It sees what is happening in any given moment and thus is not enmeshed in your thoughts, feelings, sensations and experiences. Even if there are no thoughts in your head, you exist! To discover this is the beginning of reconnecting with the meadow of your being.

You, like most everybody else, have lost sight of the truth that you are that which can see and be with what is going on. Instead, you were taught to identify with your thoughts and the sensations and feelings they generate. You then were conditioned to fight what you are experiencing, trying to make it different than what it is. You learned how to resist what is showing up in your life, especially what is uncomfortable, through evaluating, judging and trying to control your experience. But the truth is that denying, resisting, manipulating and wanting your life to be different only causes more struggle and makes your cloud bank denser.

Ask yourself, "Has this approach of constantly trying to get to the good stuff and get rid of the bad stuff ever brought you lasting peace?" If you were honest with yourself, you would have to say, "No." Imagine watching a person who is busy trying to control the movement of the clouds all day long. You can see how exhausting it is and you can see that no matter how hard they try, it doesn't work. They just get more frustrated and despairing. You can also see that they are so busy with the clouds, they don't notice the rest of Life!

If you start looking at the stories that your cloud bank tells itself, you will see that at their core there is an inner heaviness which you listen to all day long. You may secretly fear that you are not good enough or you will fail. You may experience anxiety, shame and unease. You may be afraid people will judge you, take advantage of you, or stop loving you. And you, like most people, want to be in control and are addicted to approval.

Yes, you have happy moments, kind moments and delightful moments, but they quickly go away when something happens that the mind doesn't like, for you believe that your happiness depends on the events and circumstances of your life. And yes, most of the time your storyteller just struggles with everyday things, but when a major challenge comes along, because it is so used to reacting to life, it usually doesn't know how to respond and gather the gifts that are always inherent in challenges. None of this is to be judged. This is just the way the ordinary human mind functions.

If, instead of judging, you really look, you will see that your greatest suffering comes from buying into the struggles in your mind. For the only problems you have are in your mind. Yes, you have challenges, but the mind turns them into problems and then chews on them like a cow chews her cud. Your suffering also comes from resistance to experiencing what you are actually experiencing. All resistance does is thicken your cloud bank! The more you resist your experience, the tighter you get inside, and the more you get caught in your mind, finding yourself cut off from Life.

-Ω- Close your eyes and notice that you are sitting. You are not running, taking a shower, or standing in line at the post office. All of the millions of moments of your life have brought you to this moment in which you are reading this book. Ask yourself, "How do I know that I am sitting?" Can you feel the place where your buttocks meet the chair? Is there pressure there? Is there maybe a tingle or a pain? Do not discount the power of just a moment or two of recognizing exactly what you are experiencing.

Did you pause for a few moments and give yourself your own attention? Know that this is one of the most powerful things you can give to yourself. If you didn't, just notice how strong that urge is to be anywhere except here with ourselves.

Addiction to Fixing:

One of the mind's favorite games for staying distracted and far away from what you are experiencing is to create problems and then try to figure out how to fix them. In fact, it could be said that your storyteller is a problem factory, churning out problems all day long. It is astounding to recognize that once it solves one problem, there is usually a very short period of time before it comes up with another problem, and that is what fills most people's lives. We are problem-fixer addicts!

How does this affect your life? Imagine yourself back in the meadow. Then imagine yourself sitting in the meadow engulfed with clouds, holding a completely tangled ball of yarn, with your whole focus on trying to unravel it! You aren't available to the meadow. You don't even see it. Instead, you are lost in the problem factory of your mind, trying to fix the latest problem.

In the problem factory, you are constantly trying to manipulate the world so it won't show up in ways that bring up the fear-based beliefs of your storyteller. You try to change your mate so he or she doesn't make you uncomfortable. You will stay in abusive relationships because you're afraid of experiencing the feeling of being alone. You will not get up from a meeting early, even if you have to go to the bathroom, because you can't face the fear of people judging you if you leave. Your problem factory may spend lots of money on your hair, exercise programs, diet products and maybe even plastic surgery, all in hopes that you will be accepted (and thus won't feel rejected).

Has all of this fixing and changing ever brought you the happiness you long for? Maybe it has brought you temporary happiness, but in the long run, if you look closely, you will see that the answer is, "No." When you fix one problem, the mind inevitably comes up with another! And yet, trying to fix the problem factory is only more fixing! Expecting your mind to be different is like expecting a dog to act like a cat. Instead, all we need to do is become curious about what is going on.

It is also important to understand that, even though you have been taught to believe that your mind is in charge of life, it was not designed for this. It is an exquisite tool for *maneuvering through* your life, but it is not supposed to be *in charge of* it. Life is in charge of your life, and it does a lot better job than your mind does. In fact, all of the violence, hatred and aggression on our planet have been created by people who were lost in the cloud banks of their minds, acting from fear, greed, reaction and judgment.

Giving your mind the task of being in charge of your life is like giving a child the keys to a car. Children are so small that even if they could get the car to move, they couldn't see where they were going! That is what it is like to give your mind the task of being in charge of Life. It is like driving down the road of Life blind, because you truly can't see what is going on right now, much less what is going to happen next! Giving your mind the task of being in charge of your life has twisted it into knots of neuroses, and when you see this, it makes sense as to why we are such a depressed, disconnected and addicted society.

The truth is, Life isn't under your control. For heaven's sake, you can't get your thoughts to be the way you want them to be for more than a few minutes, and yet you think that the constantly changing world of your mind is what should be in control of Life! It is so changeable that at one moment it will tell you, "Yes, let's do that." And in the next it says, "No, don't!"

You can learn how to use your mind to be curious about Life rather than always trying to control it, and you can learn how to stop arguing with Life. One of the greatest joys of awakening is to realize that you don't need to control Life. The joy and freedom that you long for come from connecting with it!

-Ω- Let go of reading the book and bring the finger of your attention to the circle of your breath, becoming very curious about what your breath is like right now. Do you feel it in your nose or in your chest? Does your belly move when you breathe? Do your arms move? Just be curious about Life expressing through you as your breath. What is your storyteller doing as you are invited to notice your breath?

The Opposite of Fixing - Curiosity:

A deep and nourishing connection with Life comes when you can see through your addiction to trying to change yourself and change your life. As long as you are trying to change something, you are caught in the cloud bank of struggle, cut off from a direct experience of Life. True and lasting healing doesn't come when you're lost in trying to fix a problem. Or as Einstein once said, "You cannot solve a problem from the same consciousness that created it. You must learn to see the world anew."

That is what we are exploring here – how to tease your attention out of the problem factory of your mind so you can use it to see your experience anew with the fresh eyes of your curiosity! The more you become curious about what is going on right now rather than trying to make things be different than what they are, the more you will get to know your storyteller and the more you will be able to unhook from its stories.

The most powerful tool you have for seeing and seeing through your clouds is your focused attention. What do I mean by that? This is when your attention and your immediate experience are together so you can see through your storyteller and your attention can come back to what is showing up in your life – not a story about it, but the real thing. It is discovering how to be honest with yourself about what your mind, your body and your emotions are doing in any given moment. It is about experiencing what you are experiencing before you think about it.

With the honesty of curiosity, you can learn how to watch the storyteller in your head without identifying with whatever story it's running at that moment. For example, when your storyteller is caught in a spell of fear, you can move from saying, "I am afraid" to "This is a story of fear." You can also use curiosity to be with emotional pain. Without falling into it or suppressing it, you can name it such as: "a ball of tears in my chest." You can even use curiosity to explore physical pain rather than trying to get away from it.

When you learn how to have a direct experience of what you are experiencing through your ability to be honest with yourself about what you are actually experiencing, you discover how to clear your cloud bank through the phenomenal power of curiosity. If your mind were a 12 cylinder car, your addiction to fixing and changing is like using only one cylinder while curiosity accesses all 12!

What we are talking about here is the ability to *relate to* what you are experiencing rather than *relate from* it. This is why I love to use the word curiosity so much. The focused attention of curiosity is about rediscovering your natural inquisitiveness. This kind of curiosity isn't about gaining knowledge. It is about accessing *knowing* by directly looking at what is happening right now. I like to call it *knowticing*, putting together the two words 'knowing' and 'noticing'!

When you realize that most of the time you are caught in ideas about Life, and then discover how to be curious instead (which is what we are exploring in this book), you begin to see that your focused attention transforms things. Your attention is like the sun: it can dispel even the deepest of states that have been bound up inside of you. The states that you are so afraid of – like fear, despair, anger and shame – are just trapped energy that you have been trying to get away from your whole life. They are like a bear in the woods. If you run away from the bear, it will run after you. If you stand and face the bear, (unless you are between a mother and her cubs) the chances are the bear will leave.

Just like with the bear, when you try to get away from the states you deem uncomfortable and unacceptable inside of you, they pursue you, taking over your life, often leading to depression and anxiety. When you turn and give them your full attention, this gives them the spaciousness they need to pass through you like the clouds in the sky. Every time you do this for a moment here and a moment there, you open yourself a little more to the flow of Life.

The last thing the mind wants to do is to experience what you are experiencing. In fact, the mind is the place you go to hide from experience for it is a masterful denial machine. It will do almost anything not to experience what is happening inside of you. It will stay busy. It will daydream and it will distract itself with iPods, iPads and TV. It is addicted to judging itself, lost in the endless game of trying to make itself better. It also loves to make other people responsible for its feelings, and it even indulges in compulsions that could kill it, all in order not to experience what it is experiencing!

Through the power of your own curiosity, you can see what your mind is doing rather than being caught in its conditioned stories of struggle. You also can discover that the safest thing you will ever do is turn toward your experience rather than turning away. The mind is afraid of this at the beginning. It is afraid that if it lets go of trying to control its experience and looks at it instead, then either something bad will happen or nothing will happen at all. That is just the fear-based mind talking.

-Ω- Put down the book and connect with the circle of your breath for a few minutes. Whenever you notice you are paying attention to your storyteller again, be curious whether your stories are about the past or the future.

When you stop arguing with Life and instead become present for your own experience, you come into alignment with your life. This is where the cloud bank of fear and control thins, for when you learn how to be fully present with the spells that you have been operating under, it becomes easier and easier to unhook from them and to let them pass right through you. The more you unhook, the more the wisdom and support of the meadow of your being become accessible. You then know again the joy and the ease of showing up for your life, allowing it to unfold through you rather than always trying to control it.

Nothing to Be Ashamed of:

Before you learn how to use your curiosity to transform your cloud bank of struggle, it is essential to understand that there is nothing inside of you to be ashamed of or afraid of. First of all, the stories that pass through your mind all day long and that fuel your feelings are all stories you learned from your environment when you were very young.

Remember, at one time there were no thoughts in your head. When you showed up out of mystery as an infant, you had no ideas about Life – none at all. You experienced Life by feeling it, and the unconscious giants that were your parents were full of every feeling a person can have – anger, sadness, fear, love, confusion, judgment, kindness, jealousy, shame, etc. Just as you learned language by listening to it, you learned the language of unconsciousness by feeling it.

What does that look like? You were wide open to Life when you were little and you could feel what was happening inside of the people around you. For example, if your parents were arguing down in the basement and you were up in the attic, you could feel what they were experiencing even though you couldn't hear them. You couldn't usually make sense of it, but you experienced it. What you were absorbing from the adults around you became the building blocks of your view of yourself and of Life, and this view was fully formed by the time you were six.

Did you have a choice of the verbal language you learned when you were young? No. If you lived in Japan you learned Japanese. If you lived in France you learned French. In the same way, if you lived in an unconscious family, as most of us did, you absorbed the language of unconsciousness that is based on fear, glued together with judgment, and has at its foundation the despair of feeling separate and alone.

Your view of Life was formed by what you absorbed from the inner world of your parents and also by what they said and did. At times they acted in ways that truly confused you. You noticed everything when you were young, including the times when what they said and what they were feeling were different. They would yell at you, saying they were not angry. They would tell you to be kind and then talk about people behind their backs. They would say that they loved you, but oftentimes would ignore or shame you when you were in need of connection.

There was so much happening around and inside of you as you were growing up, and mostly you were on your own to try to understand it all. You, like most children, probably didn't have adults around you who could help you be with what you were experiencing. So over time more and more feelings were not able to pass through you. Instead they became frozen inside of you, cutting you off from the flow of Life. Out of this disconnect and confusion, you retreated into your mind, getting lost in your storyteller that is always trying to manage what is going on.

The foundation of your stories was built out of the view of a child that was trying to make sense of the world and protect itself. But children don't have the perspective to discern what is truly going on, so they add two and two together and came up with 22. For example, one of the most common stories at the core of your child-made-me is that you were to blame for anything that was unpleasant in your family. Because children are the center of their own world, when uncomfortable and scary things happen, all they can assume is that they are the ones to blame. There was a study done once of children who went through a divorce. Up to the age of 12, even if they were told they didn't cause the divorce, they secretly felt that they had.

Another core story of your child-made-me is the spell that Life is not safe. It was big and scary and it bruised you and abandoned you over and over again. So you began to try to gain some control over this constantly changing river of Life in order not to feel the deep fear of being overwhelmed or abandoned. Over time this urge to control that is based on fear became what we are calling the storyteller, the voice inside of your head that is always talking, always trying to *do* life and *do it right* so it doesn't have to feel the deep fear and despair that is always there underneath its everyday awareness. The more you came to believe that the storyteller was who you are, the more disconnected you became from yourself and from Life.

There is another piece of information that is important to know in order not to be ashamed of what you will see when you start really looking at what you are experiencing. It is that you are not alone in being nutty as a fruitcake! We all took on the unconsciousness of our parents, just as they did from their parents, and so on and so forth all the way back through the eons of history. This also happened to your friends, your loved ones, your next-door neighbors, etc. At this point in our evolution, everybody takes on the craziness of unconsciousness.

To get a sense of what I am talking about here, imagine that when you were born you showed up in a huge warehouse that was filled with piles of Lego pieces sorted by shape, size and color. Each pile represented an aspect of the human mind, like self-judgment, sadness, happiness, loneliness, rage, kindness, anxiety, exuberance, doubt, hope, or skepticism.

Your job was to build a Lego ship (the storyteller in your head) and the only requirement was that you had to take at least one Lego from each pile. The result was that inside of you (like everybody else) are all the variations of anger, fear, grief and shame that make up our storytellers. Each person puts their Lego ship together differently, so you may have more sadness than anger, more grief than fear or more kindness than meanness. But everything a human being is capable of is inside of you.

Most people crawl into their Lego ship and it drives them through Life. What you are being invited to do is space walks! You are discovering how to step out of the Lego ship of your storyteller and look at it, so you can unhook from its stories. One of the reasons why I offer groups and retreats is so people can discover a place where they can be real and thus find out that everybody else has felt whatever they are feeling at some time in their life, and may even be feeling it right now!

So, there is absolutely nothing to be ashamed of inside of you. Yes, you have made mistakes in your life, but mistakes are just 'mis-takes' coming from the cloudiness of your storyteller, and they deserve to be forgiven. Remember, the foundational spells (beliefs) out of which your cloud bank operates were created inside of you before you were six! Yes, your cloud bank has been remodeled over the years, but the foundations are the same. Also, if you are willing to look at the spells that make up your storyteller without judgment, they will become the fuel for your awakening. Finally, you are not alone in how 'crazy' your cloud bank is. Contrary to appearances, everybody else has the same neurotic storyteller inside of them, too.

> -Ω- Take a moment and ask yourself, "What is showing up right now?" Allow your experience to reveal itself like a Polaroid picture developing. Whatever you notice, say to yourself, "I am okay just as I am." See what your storyteller does with that statement.

Nothing to Be Afraid of:

The only power your storyteller's beliefs have over you comes from your unwillingness to look at them. At the beginning, however, none of us want to look. It is like we are children hiding under our blankets because we thought we saw a monster in the closet. What you are being invited to do is to come out from under the blankets of your cloud bank so you can look at your immediate experience and discover none of it is a monster!

When you first come out from underneath the blanket of your resistance, you may still have your hands over your eyes. When you discover the courage to peak through your fingers to see actually what is going on inside of you, you begin to see that maybe the parts that you are afraid of aren't monsters at all. As you drop your hands and really look, you see that these parts are nothing more substantial than a pile of clothing that was thrown into your closet that looks like a monster.

The deep feelings you have run away from your whole life are just like that, too. They are just the mirage of something you were conditioned to be afraid of. Having been raised in terror, and having this terror affect my life for decades, I can tell you from experience that as I turned and looked at the terror, I discovered it truly was nothing to be afraid of!

As you begin even to contemplate the art of experiencing what you are experiencing, it can be scary. You have been completely brainwashed into the belief that if you just don't look, the uncomfortable and unacceptable parts of yourself will go away. But, as you have discovered, they don't. All the feelings that you stuffed inside of yourself are still there, influencing you from underneath your everyday awareness.

You usually experience them as a low-grade sense of unease, but sometimes they come roaring up at the most inopportune times, engulfing you with their energy. Then that becomes more fuel for the belief that if you let the cat out of the bag – if you actually allow yourself to experience what you are experiencing – then you will be taken over by your feelings. But the opposite is true. Curiosity is your sacred talisman, for when you are curious about what you are experiencing, you are relating to it rather than from it. The more you do this, the less you will fall into your spells.

For a long time in your life it was important to stay in denial and keep these feelings at bay. You didn't have the skills that were needed for bringing your attention to your immediate experience rather than becoming lost in it. But as you learn the skill of being curious about what is going on inside, you can be with these feelings without becoming caught in them. That is what they need in order to be transformed back into the free flowing aliveness that you are.

Yes, it takes courage to face and embrace what Life is giving you, but this is how you come back to Life. To know the joy of directly experiencing Life, you have to be able to feel what you are feeling and bring it the light of your accepting attention in order for it to let go. This is a grand adventure of opening what has been closed inside of you so your energy can flow freely again and you can know the joy of being alive. As you understand what we are exploring here, the intent of your life changes from orchestrating your life in order to feel good to the intent to experiencing your life fully – including what feels good and what doesn't.

It is important to know this isn't just about feeling what you are feeling. When most people try to feel what they feel, they get lost in what they are feeling, identifying with it. We tried that for years without much success in bringing forth lasting healing. This was seen in the Primal Scream movement of the 1970's, which believed that if we just screamed out our anger it would be released. It didn't work and thus you don't hear about Primal Scream any more. What we are talking about is meeting what you are feeling. Yes, there are feelings there, but you are bearing witness to them rather than falling into their stories.

You also begin to realize that trying to feel good is like chasing the pot of gold at the end of the rainbow. You may think you capture it at times, but it always seems to slip away. However, when you are willing to let go of trying to make your life be a particular way and instead open to what Life is giving you, to feel what you are really feeling without getting lost in stories, you begin to know joy. You may experience happiness for awhile in getting what you think you want, but joy is the ability to be with whatever is!

-Ω- Is your storyteller liking or disliking what it is reading?

Your Body as Your Friend:

What we are exploring here is the alchemy of attention. We used to believe that alchemy was about changing lead into gold. True alchemy is about transforming unconsciousness into consciousness. It is about discovering how to *relate to* what you are experiencing rather than *from* it through being curious about what is going on right now. Learning how to dip the finger of your attention into the river of your experience will change your life. You will be much less a victim to what is happening and more able to transform your experience through the power of focused attention.

Like most people, the muscle of your attention is probably flaccid. Your attention has been caught inside of your mind for so long, being pulled from one thought to another all day long that you have lost the ability simply to be curious about what is happening right now. So in each of the Re-membering Sessions, we have been flexing your muscle of attention so that it becomes strong enough that you can be curious about what is going on right now.

This is where your journey back to yourself becomes very interesting. You discover the joy of actually being present for yourself. Whether you know it or not, this is what you have been longing for most of your life – to have your attention and your immediate experience together! It is about *being with* what you are experiencing rather than just thinking about it.

We started strengthening your attention in the Re-membering Sessions by being curious about the circle of your breath. You were then connected to the power of deepening your breath through the candle breath and bringing calm through the calming/focusing words. The next step was to discover how to watch your storyteller by noticing whether it is telling stories about the past or the future.

Now it is time to deepen your ability to experience what you are truly experiencing by being in your body, for most of the time you are not there. You are caught in your head and see the body as just a vehicle for carrying it around! But your body is one of the best friends you have on the journey back to Life. It is full of wisdom and will tell you exactly what you are experiencing long before your mind will. It is communicating its wisdom to you all of the time, but you were not taught how to listen.

Let's take a moment to listen:

> -Ω- Bring your attention to your body for just a minute or two and find three distinctly different sensations. Don't rush this. It is like allowing a Polaroid picture to develop. Just be curious and the sensations will reveal themselves. You could notice warmth, cold, tingles, throbbing, stabbing, aching, lightness, pressing, fullness, hunger, etc. Name to yourself what you are noticing. Again, your attention at times will drift back into your storyteller. No reason to judge this. Simply notice you're caught in your mind again and bring your attention back to your body. When you are ready, resume reading the book.

Did you pause and connect with your body? If you didn't, no judgment. You have only spent most of your life far away from the wisdom and joy of your own body. However, do acknowledge your resistance. If you did turn your attention toward your body, your mind may very well have become bored because it is used to the manic activity of your storyteller. So you may have wandered off, thinking about the past or the future or, after a few seconds, just wanted to get on with reading the book. But know that every time you bring your attention back to the sensations of your body, you are clearing a pathway from the cloudbank of your mind into the meadow of your beingness.

What we are talking about is one of the most healing things a human being can do. To feel your way into your body is to open into a field of joy and aliveness for which you are homesick. Turning your attention to your body will also allow you to be more intimate with yourself, discovering that your body is speaking to you at all times and its wisdom is amazing. This will help you to see more clearly what stories you are running in your head rather than being at their mercy, for your spells express as patterns of holding in your body. The more you look, the more you will be able to unhook from what you formerly thought of as true. Curiosity is where magic happens. My first teacher taught me, "In the seeing is the movement." He showed me that you don't need to fix, change, get rid of or judge your stories. All you need to do is see them and see that they really are just spells you took on when you were very young that show up as the storyteller in your head, generating sensations and feelings.

The more you watch your experience with curiosity, the more you discover how to unhook from the spells of your storyteller – the foundational spells of: "I am separate from Life" and "Life is not safe". This allows you to get to know the three operational spells of: "I must *do* Life". "I must *do* it right" and "I am not *doing* it right enough". This brings you to the three hidden spells: (Because I am not doing it right) "I am wrong;" "I am unlovable;" "I am all alone."

The more you get to know your storyteller, the more these spells will simply pass through you, and the more easily you will see that only a small part of who you are is struggling with Life. The rest of you is at peace. This is the meadow of your being that is always with you right here, right now.

RE-MEMBERING SECTION

Re-membering Session

Now you have a greater ability to bring your attention into this moment through grounding it in your breath. You can also more easily see what your storyteller is doing through recognizing whether it is telling stories of the past or the future. So it is time to deepen your ability to be present for yourself through feeling your way into your body, exploring what you are experiencing in different areas. This is about having your attention and your immediate experience together. As you explore, you will see how far away from your body you usually are. You will also see how, when your attention is fully with what you are actually experiencing, holdings in your body can begin to open up.

Remember, you are not trying to make anything happen here. You are not even trying to meditate. All you are doing is being curious about your immediate experience by bringing your attention to your body. This is what I mean when I call it *knowticing*, which is the art of using your attention to notice what is happening without trying to make anything happen. In this kind of noticing, knowing can arise.

Read through these instructions and then put the book down and begin exploring. If timing your session, add one minute, taking it to nine minutes. Trust yourself on the amount of time. If nine minutes is too much, shorten it a bit. If time is not an issue, stay with each step as long as your curiosity is engaged.

Let's begin:

- Close your eyes and dip the finger of your attention into the river of your experience, noticing what it is like to be you right now.

- For at least three in-breaths, tighten your muscles and then very slowly relax everything on your out-breath as you say the great sound of letting go, "Ahh!"

- Bring your attention to the circle of your breath, saying the calming/focusing words, "In...Out; Deep...Slow; Calm...Ease."

Now bring your attention to a place in your body that interests you. It could be a place where the energy is open, generating wonderful sensations, or it could be a place of holding. If no place is calling to you, bring your attention to a place where you chronically hold tension. Rather than turning away from it, turn toward it, being curious about what is happening in this area. There are many sensations happening there and they are like creatures in the forest. If you sit quietly, they will reveal themselves to you. Be patient and, just as a Polaroid picture slowly reveals itself, they will appear through the light of your attention.

Here are some questions to keep your curiosity activated:

- What am I experiencing here?

- How big is it?

- What is the nature of the sensations: aching, throbbing, tingling, etc?

- Do the sensations move around or stay the same?

- Is it on the surface or deeper in my body?

These questions are designed to invite your attention to be curious about exactly what is going on in this area. As you allow your attention to settle there, many different sensations will reveal themselves. Be curious! Whenever you find your attention has wandered back to your storyteller, bring it back to this area and be fascinated about what you can discover.

Now gently breathe into this area. Touch this holding from the inside with your own breath, allowing the touch to be as soft as a mother's caress.

Stay with this exploration as long as it interests you. It may be 30 seconds or a number of minutes. Don't force it, but be willing to remember that huge gifts come out of the ability to have your attention present for what is happening in your body. When you feel complete with your exploration, come back to the circle of breath and the calming/focusing words.

- For a few moments at the end, open your attention to include your whole body and notice what is different now that you have given yourself the healing of your own attention.

- When you are ready, open your eyes.

Each day you can explore another part of your body with this kind of depth. Remember, this is like developing a Polaroid picture. As your attention settles in an area, it may not seem like much is going on. But as you stay there, the full variety of sensations happening in that area will make themselves known to you. It is under the gaze of your attention that bound up energy, if it is ready, can begin to move and let go.

Abbreviated Version:

- Close your eyes and dip the finger of your attention into the river of your experience, noticing what it is like to be you right now.

- For at least three breaths, tighten your muscles and then very slowly relax everything on your out-breath as you say the great sound of letting go, "Ahh!"

- Bring your attention to the circle of your breath and the calming/focusing words.

- Now bring your attention into your body by exploring an area with great curiosity, allowing the sensations to reveal themselves. Gently breathe into them.

- When you feel complete with your exploration, come back to the circle of breath and the calming/focusing words.

- At the end, expand your awareness and be curious about your experience after having given yourself the healing of your own attention.

- When you are ready, open your eyes.

Re-memberings

- To know again the joy of being fully alive, you need to get to know your cloud bank of struggle – the spells (beliefs) it is made up of and the stories it tells when caught in its spells.

- Denying, resisting, manipulating or wanting your life to be different only deepens struggle.

- The mind resists Life by creating problems and then trying to fix them. Once it solves one problem, it comes up with another.

- You can learn how to use your mind to be curious about Life rather than trying to control it.

- The more you become curious about what is going on right now rather than always trying to change things, the more you will get to know your cloud bank and the more it will thin.

- There is nothing inside of you to be ashamed of or afraid of.

- The only power your storyteller's spells have over you comes from your unwillingness to look at them and, at least at the beginning, none of us want to look.

- You have been conditioned to believe that, if you don't look, the uncomfortable and unacceptable parts of you will go away. But they don't.

- Fully experiencing Life without the filter of our storyteller is what we all deeply long for!

- The mind is afraid of looking so it will do all sorts of things to distract you from being curious.

- As you turn your attention towards yourself, you are not trying to make anything happen. All you are doing is being curious about your immediate experience.

- As you see your spells, you will see through them, bringing your attention back to the joy of being fully here for Life, right now.

CHAPTER 6

Directly Experiencing Life

For the past five chapters we have been strengthening the muscle of your attention, inviting you to be curious about your breath, your storyteller, and your body. It is now time to bring your awakening curiosity into what is happening as you move through your day. This is where it all gets very interesting. Rather than Life being a random series of events that are happening either because you are doing it right or are doing it wrong, you begin to trust that Life is putting you in the exact situations that are needed to bring up the spells that make up your storyteller so you can see them in operation. In that powerful moment of just seeing them (*knowticing*), they lose their power over you.

I like to say it this way:

Life is set up

to bring up

what has been bound up

so it can open up

to be freed up

so you can show up

for Life!

In other words, Life is for you. Another way to say it is "What's in the way, IS the way!" Any experience that tightens you is *set up* by Life to *bring up* what has been *bound up* inside of you so these parts of yourself can begin to *open up* under the light of your curiosity. As they loosen, they begin to move through you rather than being stuck inside of you, where they cause all sorts of difficulties in your life. The more you *free up* what has been *bound up* through the light of your curiosity, your cloud bank thins and the more available you are to Life: you *show up*!

Rather than trusting Life enough that you show up for what it is offering you, you have been conditioned to resist what you are experiencing. You are in a tug of war with your own experience, and this has prevented you from recognizing the field of well-being that is always here. What we are exploring is how to let go of your end of the rope in that tug of war by not resisting what you are experiencing so you can bring it the healing power of your own curiosity.

It is through curiosity that you can begin to see the storyteller in your head that talks all day long, putting a veil between you and Life. Even though it is very seductive and seemingly very strong, it is not stronger than your ability to see it and unhook from its stories. One of the core stories to see through is the belief that you need to change your inner or outer environment in order to know the peace and well-being you long for. Nothing could be further from the truth. Nothing needs to be changed. The stories of struggle only need to be seen for what they are - stories in your head that you became lost in when you were young.

Through the honesty of curiosity, you discover how to transform the struggles of your storyteller into the free-flowing aliveness that is your natural state, just as the sun dispels the morning fog. Think of a time where a major problem in your life was suddenly solved. Can you remember how light and energized you became? It was as if a 100-pound weight had been lifted from your heart. That 100-pound weight is your storyteller who keeps on creating problems and contracting around its struggles. Rather than being a victim to your life, through curiosity you can learn to unhook from the stories as they are happening, no matter what is happening in your life. As you unhook more and more from your storyteller, you discover the field of well-being that is always with you.

-Ω- Allow one, long deep in-breath and say the sound "Ahh" as you are breathing out.

The You-Turn:

What we are exploring is the art of showing up for your Life rather than trying to make it be what you think it should be. We have been trained to believe Life is happening to us and we must control it. This only leads to an endless game of struggle. Instead, you can begin to recognize that Life is for you. As you do, you discover that it is putting you into the exact situations you need in order to see the spells you took on.

In learning how to show up for what Life is offering you, it helps to become what I call a 'tightness detective.' Instead of being upset about being upset, you become curious. Whenever you are identified with the spells that make up your storyteller, you tighten. Your body tightens, your heart tightens and so does your mind, dimming the free-flowing aliveness that you are. Tightening is signaling you to become curious about what you are experiencing. Whenever you are tightening, it is a guarantee that there is something you are resisting, so you become alert to the times you tighten. Rather than getting lost in all of the stories that are running through your head, you turn toward your experience, giving your stories the acknowledgement they need to let go.

Let's say you are at work and your boss comes in and is upset with you about something you have or haven't done. In the past, you may have fallen into a story of "I'm not smart enough." Or you thought, "He is a horrible boss." You may have reacted by becoming immobile like a deer in the headlights or argued with your boss or just took it on and then talked to your friends about what a horrible boss you have. All of these reactions keep what was triggered stuck inside of you. But now, after your boss leaves, you notice that you are tight. Instead of being a victim to the experience and distracting yourself, you find the willingness to be curious instead.

I call what we are exploring here the 'you-turn.' When faced with something that brings up discomfort inside of them, most people spend their energy on reacting, blaming, fixing or running away. But this never heals anything in the long run. It is a gigantic leap in your awakening when you realize that your suffering does not come from what is happening in your life. Suffering comes from your stories about what is happening. People who have gone through great suffering and emerged empowered did so because they were able to see through the stories of victimhood and instead showed up for what Life was giving them.

A good friend who had been incorporating the you-turn in little upsets in her life told me of a time where she and her husband had a very heated argument. In the middle of it she was caught in her spells. Both the feeling of being a victim was there, along with the urge to attack him! But her reactions woke up her curiosity and she excused herself. When she went into the other room, she sat quietly and simply watched her storyteller go wild with stories. One moment the storyteller said she was going to leave him and made a list of all of the reasons why. In the next moment she was afraid he would leave her! She didn't buy into any of these stories. Instead she just watched and slowly the stories wound down and she and her husband were able to communicate clearly.

It does take time to unhook at the level that she did, but that is the power of the 'you-turn.' It is about bringing your attention back to yourself, especially when you find yourself getting tight, so that you can recognize your stories and the sensations and feelings they generate. It is when you can see what is going on inside of you that you can give these parts the attention they need to let go. For it is 'a given' that if you are tightening, there is a part of your spell that is activated and needs your attention. Every time you turn your attention toward what you are experiencing, your cloud bank thins, and it becomes easier to connect with the meadow of Life.

-Ω- Dip the finger of your attention into the river of your experience and simply notice what you notice. This moment matters.

The Wisdom of Your Body:

You spent time exploring your body in the last chapter because it is your GPS system for life. If you listen, it will tell you exactly what is going on inside of you. Every single story and the feelings it generates are expressed in your body in a particular way, and your body will signal you, long before your mind will, that you are reacting to something. You may notice that your heart is pounding, or there is a lump in your throat, or maybe a fist in your solar plexus. You might also notice a cramp in your neck, a heavy weight on your chest, or a hollow feeling in your belly.

All of these are physical reactions that are manifestations of the stories and feelings that were awakened through a particular encounter. Every pattern of holding in your body is an expression of one of the spells of your storyteller. That cramp in your neck could be an expression of "I didn't do it right". That fist in your stomach may be deep fear that you don't know how to do it right. The hollow feeling in your belly could be a manifestation of the fear of being rejected and thus all alone. All of these stories/feelings that have been with you since you were young keep on showing up in your life because they need to receive the healing of your accepting attention. Your sensations, and the thoughts and feelings that are fueling them, are just like you: they want to be heard. Let's do a little exploring:

-Ω- Bring your attention to your face and ask yourself, "How do I know I have a face?" In other words, what are the sensations happening right now in my face? Are there tingles there? Maybe an itch? Possibly a slight headache? Perhaps some pressure? Find at least three different sensations. When you are complete, come back to the book.

In these few moments, you were invited to feel what your body was actually experiencing: not an idea about it, but the actual, living experience of it. Of course there may be resistance initially to experiencing your face, for your storyteller is not accustomed to being curious. When I notice that my storyteller has taken over again and is resistant to being curious about what is happening in my body, I tell it, "I know you want to stay in charge, but being present for what is right now is where the good stuff is!" My mind has finally seen that when full attention is brought to my actual experience, especially something that I have been resisting, a doorway opens and the bound up energy releases. So when I remind my storyteller that this is where the good stuff is, it usually lets go and I can again be fully with whatever is happening right now.

One of the most powerful feedback systems you have in your body is your belly. When your belly is holding on, it is because you are caught in your storyteller. When you come back to the meadow, your belly automatically softens. If you pay attention, your tight belly will signal you that you are believing the stories in your head again. And softening the belly is a gentle reminder to your storyteller that it can let go.

-Ω- Bring your attention to your belly. Is it soft and open? If it is holding, on the next in-breath tighten it, and then slowly let it go on the out-breath.

To develop the willingness to listen to your body so it can show you the stories that you got caught in, it can be helpful to give yourself the gift of noticing your body before you get out of bed each morning. If you honestly ask yourself what you are experiencing, you will discover that you have different sensations every day. One day your shoulder may be cold or your feet hot. Your back may ache one morning and not the next. You may feel rested or tired, hungry or not, peaceful or agitated, contented or anxious. Every moment you actually experience your body is a moment of strengthening your curiosity.

Deepening Curiosity:

It does take time to develop curiosity about what you are actually experiencing and you may only be able to be this curious about your reactions in situations that don't carry much charge for you, like during some of your Re-membering Sessions. You can also do the you-turn while watching TV or at a movie theater. Be curious about what your storyteller is saying and what kind of sensations and feelings it is generating. You can also do this while riding the bus, waiting in line at the Post Office or even when you are put on an interminably long hold on the phone.

When you start to be able to bring curiosity into more challenging situations of your life, you may only be able to do this awhile after you have been triggered. It doesn't matter if it is a couple of hours or a couple of months later. With a short delay, the cascades of reactions are still happening and you can bring your attention to them. If it is days, weeks or months later, you can go back in your imagination and meet with your attention what is brought up inside of you. The more you do this, the more you will be able to do it right after a challenging situation and then right in the middle of one. That is freedom.

In order to sharpen curiosity, at different moments throughout your day you can ask yourself, "What is my storyteller saying right now?" At first you may not be able to notice anything for, if you are like most people, you have been lost inside of your storyteller for most of your life. At the beginning, to ask what your storyteller is saying can feel like asking somebody to describe the outside of a house that they have never left. But keep on asking anyway, for that level of curiosity will begin to open doors that allow you to step outside of the "house" of your storyteller, becoming able to relate to what it is saying, rather than from it. If that question doesn't call to you, here are some others that will invite you into the healing of a you-turn:

- What is tightening in my body right now?
- What is it like to be me right now?
- What sits here right now?
- Without changing anything, what is showing up right now?

Remember, with this kind of question you are not trying to find an answer with your mind or make something go away. You are using these questions to wake up your curiosity so that your attention and your immediate experience can meet. That is where alchemy can happen. When you notice something, whether it is a sensation, a story or a feeling, name what you see. This is what we were doing when you named whether you were drifting off into the past or the future.

The most basic naming is "story." But as you develop your capacity to see what is going on, you will be able to be more specific about what you see – fear, sadness, planning, spacing out, irritation, boredom, to name a few. At the beginning you may be confused about exactly what you are experiencing. So confusion is what you are experiencing and you can then say, "Confusion!"

When you name something, you are *relating to* what you are experiencing rather than being caught in it or resisting it. This is a moment of freedom, and each moment counts. For most people, being identified with their storyteller is like being in a wind tunnel with the 10,000-piece picture puzzle of their various spells flying all around. Not much fun. At moments you may be happy about floating around, but then a puzzle piece hits you in the eye and it hurts! You are being shown that you don't have to stay in the wind tunnel of your mind. Through curiosity you can step out of it and then discover how to stick your hand back into the tunnel to grab a piece of the puzzle here and there.

To name whatever you are experiencing is like looking at the piece of the puzzle you have taken out of the wind tunnel and then putting it on the table in front of you. Every moment of seeing and naming what you are actually experiencing is another step in putting the puzzle together. You may not be able yet to see where it goes in the puzzle, but that will become clearer as you deepen your ability to be curious. Slowly, piece by piece, the entire puzzle of your storyteller becomes apparent. This is where you can clearly see the spells upon which your storyteller bases its world of struggle. In that clarity, whatever pattern you are noticing won't have as much power to draw you back into the wind tunnel of struggle.

As you learn how to experience directly what you are experiencing, know that resistance will be a part of it. In fact, you could say that resistance and the cloud bank of struggle mean the same thing! You have spent most of your life resisting what you are experiencing. Your mind may want to argue with that, but if you look closely, you will see that mostly you live in ideas about what you are experiencing and not the real thing.

Resistance is all about getting as far away from your experience as you can for your storyteller wants to stay in control by not looking. No need to judge or fight that. You, and everyone else, learned very early on that the only way you could stop being overwhelmed by painful experiences was to resist them by tightening your body, holding your breath, and not looking. This caused you to retreat to your mind and, for most of your life, to unconsciously resist anything that is confusing, uncomfortable or scary, keeping you lost in the spells of your storyteller.

But you no longer have to get lost in resistance and *you don't have to resist your resistance*! Instead you can have a direct experience of it. Like all feelings, it has a story, along with an emotional component that is unique, and it shows up in your body in a particular way. However you notice it, acknowledge that it is here. Then you can ask the resistance, "What is it that you are taking care of?" If something reveals itself, great. If not, then continue on with your life, but remember that this kind of question sets things in motion and Life will show you what is asking to be seen when you are ready for it.

> -Ω- Pause for a moment and ask "What is my storyteller saying right now?" Name whatever you notice. If you are not clear, say "story" and then return to reading.

Discomfort:

To discover the transformative power of having your attention and your immediate experience together, you need to change your relationship to discomfort. To be fully awake to Life means showing up for both the easy and the difficult, the joyous and the sorrowful. For the truth is that to be open to Life means experiencing pain. It hurts to break your leg, or get the flu or even stub your toe. And everybody you love will die before you or you will die before them.

If you are like most people, you love to show up for the easy, but are not at all comfortable with showing up for the difficult. It is important to understand that you turn your pain into suffering when you resist it. In fact, it is in discomfort that you most often leave yourself for the world of struggle. So it could be said that you leave yourself when you most need yourself!

It becomes a lot easier to stay open to Life when you learn how not to tighten around discomfort, for all that does is increase your cloud bank! To soften around discomfort, whether it is physical, mental or emotional, allows it to pass through you much more quickly.

Along with happiness, pleasure and comfort, there is a lot of discomfort in life: illness, traffic jams, rejection, irritation, financial challenges, pain in your back, anxiety, big thighs, loss, shame. Every day you are either feeling discomfort or trying to get away from it. This happens on the physical level and even more on the mental and emotional levels.

We carry so much pain inside of us. First, there is our body that is usually expressing some discomfort somewhere. When you begin checking into your body, you will be amazed at how much chronic tightness you carry around with you all day long.

My niece, Jody Stanislaw, in her book *Hunger*, wrote about an experience she had around chronic tension at a 10-day silent meditation retreat. In the morning meditation on day eight, she was supposed to be doing a body scan. Instead, her body began to spontaneously move. Part of her thought she should stop these movements and get back to practicing the meditation technique. But she made the choice of allowing this to happen, enjoying seeing where and how her body wanted to move. She said it felt as if her muscles were literally unwinding. After the meditation, she clasped her arms behind her back and raised them in the air, something she had never been able to do. Not even an inch. And now she could raise them to a 90 degree angle.

When she wrote about this, she said, "I was amazed to realize it had taken me over a week of stillness and meditation for my muscles to fully let go. It made me acutely aware of how much tension I must hold on a daily basis. My back felt phenomenal. It was more supple and relaxed than I could ever remember it being before. I pondered how contracted we humans can be, not just physically, but mentally, too. I thought about how much suffering we generate when living in this state of self-induced contraction. I became convinced that every time I had resisted or felt pity about a fact of my life, I had created tension in my body, analogous to putting a rock into my metaphysical backpack."

The storyteller also creates tightness in our minds and emotions. There is the background noise of anxiety: "Am I doing this right?" "Will they like me?" "Do I look okay?" "What if I say the wrong thing?" There is also the emotional pain of never being loved enough and having your heart closed to yourself. Finally, there is the disconnect that comes from being lost in your conceptual world, having to think all the time.

It won't take very long in your exploration of your inner life to see that what tightens you is uncomfortable. That is why you have run away from it for so long. Your storyteller's job is to manage your discomfort so you don't have to feel it, but if you look closely, you will see that any attempt to avoid discomfort keeps you bound to it. So you walk around in your life in a low grade fever of struggle, resisting the healing fever that comes from actually experiencing what you are experiencing.

When you remember that fevers are cleansing and you feel better after they pass, you can begin to change your relationship to discomfort. Rather than something to resist, it is something to be with and explore. The more you explore, the more you recognize that discomfort is just trapped energy that needs your full attention in order to be released.

My whole life had been geared around not wanting to feel a very uncomfortable, tightly held ball of yuk in my stomach. I tried to eat it away and deny it, but it still influenced many of my actions. When I first started turning towards it with curiosity, it was like looking through thick fog. But slowly I made contact, and lo and behold, as my attention settled there, I found it was nothing to be afraid of. Not only that, I found that as I gave it my attention, this tightly held energy opened up and there was the peace I had sought for so long by trying to get rid of this feeling!

-Ω- Bring your attention to your belly again. If it is tight, there is something you are resisting. Let it soften as an invitation to experience whatever you are experiencing.

The Treasures of Discomfort:

How can you see discomfort in a new light so you don't have to tighten around it? If you step back and watch the unfolding of Life, you can see that it is made out of the opposites of dark and light, and darkness has gotten a bad rap. We are all heat-seeking missiles in search of comfort and pleasure and we mightily resist any discomfort. Has this ever brought you the peace you long for? If you were honest with yourself, you would say "Maybe for a little bit here and there but, in the long run, no."

What if you got it backwards? What if the treasures of Life that you long for are hidden within the places that you see as uncomfortable? This theme is certainly present in most every myth that has been passed down through the ages. The hero always has to go to the places that he doesn't want to go in order to get the treasure: the princess or the Holy Grail or the pot of gold.

The truth that discomfort is not the black hole you thought it was is also revealed in the yin/yang symbol, which is one of the most familiar symbols in the world. It not only shows the light and the dark nestled together, but it takes it one step further. There is a point of light in the dark and a point of dark in the light.

What would it be like to know that in the uncomfortable challenges of your life there is always a doorway into the light? In other words, your challenges are for you! They are not here because you have done something wrong, anyone else has done something wrong, or the Powers that Be fell asleep on the job! The uncomfortable challenges are the fuel for your awakening, and as soon as you can embrace the uncomfortable, a door opens inside of you.

Each of us is a mix of dark and light, and the beings that have unhooked from the game of struggle are those who have learned how to change their relationship with the difficult from resistance to curiosity and acceptance.

What we are talking about here is the theme of The Guest House, a popular poem by Rumi, a Persian poet from the 13th century. In this poem he talks about how all sorts of feelings move through us all day long, and he says that the key is not to fight them. Instead, he says:

Welcome and entertain them all!
Even if they're a crowd of sorrows,
who violently sweep your house
empty of its furniture,
still, treat each guest honorably.
He may be clearing you out
for some new delight.
Be grateful for whoever comes,
because each has been sent
as a guide from beyond.

This poem speaks to so many people because it is about the art of alchemy we are exploring here. It voices the power of letting go of resisting what we are experiencing and opening to it instead. He even goes so far as to speak the core truth of consciousness: be grateful for your discomforts because "each has been sent as a guide from beyond." Your discomforts are not here because something is wrong. They are here as your guides through the cloud bank of struggle and back into the meadow of Life.

The final gift that comes from the difficulties in your life is that the deepest darkness inside of you, which we all have, will only let go through the light of consciousness. Remember, consciousness is the ability to see and be with *what is*, without needing it to be any different than what it is. So your darkness, rather than being a mistake, is Life coming to you in a form that will show you the power of being curious about *what is* rather than the unconsciousness of fixing, changing, judging, getting rid of or rising above. In other words, your challenges are here to show you that healing isn't about stopping the game of struggle. It is about looking at it.

It is time to let go of fighting with the difficulties and discomforts of your life. This has only kept you caught in the game of struggle. It is time to learn how to explore your difficulties, understanding that discomfort is pointing you to parts of your storyteller that want to be seen and thinned so you can rediscover the meadow of Life. You can learn how to honor the difficult aspects of your life. You can experience the magic of turning toward yourself when you get triggered and listening to what is being revealed, giving your reactions the accepting attention they need to transform.

What we are exploring here is: *what's in the way IS the way*! Whatever you are experiencing is a doorway into its opposite. So rather than resisting discomfort you can learn how to open to what you are experiencing and explore it without any need to have it be any different than what it is. Being curious about your immediate experience allows your old feelings to pass through you more and more quickly, revealing the meadow of your natural state.

Imagine the absolute joy of not resisting discomfort. Imagine that even in the most difficult situations in your life, your time of reaction is very short before curiosity kicks in and you feel spacious around whatever you are experiencing. In my life, besides the joy of being open to Life again, the other greatest joy I know is to have a formerly contracted and heavy state come for a visit and not only not be afraid of it but to turn toward it and be with what I notice. In that moment, I am relating to it rather than from it and this is what dispels the spells we all took on when we were young.

It can be very helpful when you notice you are tightening to smile! There is increasing scientific evidence that with a smile, you literally change the pathways in your brain, especially when you allow the smile to fill your body. Many of your reactions will let go in the presence of a smile.

It is also helpful to breathe into the tightening. Remember, as a child you learned how to lessen your feelings by tightening your belly and holding onto your breath. To breathe into an experience allows you to open rather than to contract around it. All contraction does is keep this trapped energy bound up inside of you, and there is nothing that is worth closing around. So breathe! In my book *The Gift of Our Compulsions*, there is a wonderful chapter on how to use your breath to open what has been closed. If you don't have the book, email us at the address at the end of this book and we will send you the chapter.

So discomfort is not what it looks like on the surface. The more you open to it, the more you discover an amazing thing: you will always be fine. The only thing that bothers you is your imagined clouds. None of it is solid. They are just clouds passing through the spacious meadow of your being, and you are that which can see what is going on. The more you see what is going on, the more curious you are. The more curious you are about what is happening right now, the more the cloud bank of your struggling self thins.

-Ω- Find an area of your body where there is holding and bring the light of your attention there. As your curiosity rests there, invite it to soften. Don't force this. You are not trying to make it let go, you are inviting it.

The Five Great Teachers:

As you live your life, there are five core teachers that are designed to bring up what is most asking for the healing of your attention: compulsions, illness, pain, finances, and people. Each of these areas is full of invitations to practice the *you-turn*, spending your energy on being curious about what they bring up inside of you rather than trying to fix, change or get rid of what is going on.

Compulsions:

The first is compulsions. We are all compulsive and you can be compulsive about anything! Rather than being something that is wrong with you and needs to be controlled, your compulsion becomes something to be curious about. For whenever you are interested in turning away from yourself through a compulsion, there is a spell close to the surface of your awareness that is asking for the light of your attention. Your compulsion, rather than a problem to be solved, becomes a guide in showing you what is asking to be seen and released. You do this through your ability to be very curious, in a spacious and nonjudgmental way, about what is happening inside of you before, during and after a wave of compulsion.

Illness:

The same is true for illness. Anything that is out of balance in your body is the body asking for you to listen to it and be with it in a different way. And yet you were never taught to listen. Instead of being responsible for your experience (which is the ability to respond), you were taught to try to get rid of the discomfort through pills and surgery. And when that doesn't fully work, you (like most people) tend to numb yourself out through, food, alcohol and cigarettes, trying to make the discomfort go away. Pills and surgery do have their place, but most of the imbalances in our bodies come from the ways we attempt to resist what we are experiencing. These can be easily brought back into balance by trusting that Life is inviting us to be with ourselves in a different way and listening to that.

Pain:

The third area is the aches and pains you experience. You were taught to contract around the painful feelings inside of you. Over the years, your chronic patterns of holdings can turn into painful necks, back spasms and overly acidic stomachs. In these areas of holding in your body, if you take the time to listen to them, you can hear the spells and the feelings that are bound up there that caused you to tighten that area in the first place. In that listening, there is the possibility of becoming free from whatever spells have been tightening your body.

Finances:

The fourth area is finances, which is loaded with opportunities to fuel our storyteller and all of its spells. There is so much fear around being supported which taps into our core mistrust of Life. The underlying spell is "There is not enough." We will overwork to make sure we have what we feel is enough. We will also hoard, manipulate, gamble, lie and even steal to calm down this deep belief. Then, if all of our controlling and manipulating doesn't work, the storyteller will go into *awfulizing*, convinced something terrible will happen. This is a powerful belief to work with, and it is an invitation to take Rumi's counsel and meet the feelings of fear and dread as guests that have come to bring you the gift of awareness that there is something greater and wiser than you in charge.

People:

The final area is the people in your life. They are some of the most powerful teachers of consciousness. Yes, you have friends, family, lovers, acquaintances and co-workers. But on another level, all of the people in your life are just character actors in your theater of awakening designed to show up in ways to bring up inside of you what is asking to be seen and released. It is the people that most disturb you that are the greatest invitation to do the *you-turn*.

The more aware you become you will realize that the deepest reactions you have around other people are when their words and actions wake up one of your spells, especially if somebody says or does something that you secretly don't like about yourself. The more you don't like the part that is awakened inside of you, the deeper your reaction will be. The more you react, the more you get caught in the quicksand of blaming, controlling and defending. The more curious you are, the quicker you will unhook from your reactions.

∞

Learning the art of the *you-turn* is where you take a huge step in being responsible for your own experience. You begin to realize that most of what you experience in relationship to people, pain, illness, finances and compulsions is just your storyteller, arising from the spells you took on. In the past when you were triggered by experiences in your life, you fell into the victim mode. The more you can do the *you-turn* and become interested in what is being brought up inside you, the less reactive you are and the more quickly your reaction passes through, opening you again to the spaciousness of your heart.

> -Ω- Bring forth into your imagination one of the core challenges you are experiencing at this time in your life. Open to the possibility that this challenge is for you. Ask Life to reveal to you the treasures that are embedded in this challenge. Then let that question go to work its magic.

Curiosity and your Daily Life:

In the last two chapters we have been exploring the phenomenal power of your own focused attention that will help you see and see through the cloud bank of your mind so you can recognize the meadow of Life again. I hope you have been able to see that ignorance is not bliss. In fact, to avoid looking just keeps you caught in the world of struggle, cut off from the joy of being fully alive.

I invite you not to make curiosity another task to do in your life. That is just more of the same old system of your mind trying to *do* Life and *do it right*. Instead, I invite you to wake up each morning with a simple willingness to be curious. Be willing to experience directly what you are experiencing by being honest with yourself. Be willing to gift yourself with your Re-membering Session every day. Now is the time for you to take responsibility for your own inner world rather than getting lost in reaction, blame, shame, resistance, fear, etc. You have the choice to be curious about what is tight inside of you or to continue trying to avoid it.

To deepen curiosity in your daily life, write down some of the questions we explored above and put these little reminders in places where you will come across them numerous times throughout the day: in your wallet, on the dashboard of your car, on the bathroom mirror, on your TV.

Ask these questions when you're sitting at a stoplight, or eating your breakfast, or sitting at your computer. The more you dip the finger of your attention into the river of your experience, the more the muscle of your curiosity will strengthen. Then you will be able to live these questions when you notice you are tightening around an experience. Eventually you will be able to access curiosity no matter what is happening in your life.

The more you invite yourself to be curious, the less resistant you become to whatever you are experiencing. You are also no longer afraid of what Life may bring you for you know that even the challenges of your life are for you because they bring up inside of you whatever is asking for healing. You then live Life in a state of discovery, opening to the adventure of Life.

Yes, this takes courage. But it is important to know that the root word for courage is from Old French and it means 'of the heart.' Yes, you have been trained your whole life not to experience what you are experiencing. But I ask you, "Do you want all of the pain that was bound up inside of you stuck inside of you?" Or as Pema Chödrön says, "Do I prefer to grow up and relate to Life directly, or do I choose to live and die in fear?"

This doesn't happen overnight. It's the journey of a lifetime. But what is more important in Life than coming back to yourself, becoming yourself, giving Life the gift of being fully you? Every moment you go toward your experience rather than getting lost in it or running away from it clears more of your cloud bank so you can be fully alive.

As you are developing your curiosity, you may notice that a lot of things don't let go easily. In the next chapter we will continue our journey together by exploring the art of listening. The deepest parts of your story of struggle need to be touched by an accepting heart. As they receive the power of being welcomed rather than resisted, true alchemy happens.

RE-MEMBERING SECTION

Re-membering Session

We have been developing the muscle of your attention by bringing it first to your breath and, from this foundation, becoming curious about what your storyteller is doing (past and future). We then invited your attention into the GPS of your body for it will signal you that you are caught in your cloud bank through how it tightens and holds. This week we will develop your capacity to meet whatever you are experiencing with the compassionate curiosity it needs to heal.

There are two more words we will be adding to the end of your calming/focusing words that will invite both your attention and your heart to be with whatever you are experiencing: "As is…I'm here." So you will be silently saying on the rhythm of your breath: "In…Out; Deep…Slow; Calm…Ease; As is…I'm here." (or you can say them on their own.) Just like the other pairs of words, "As is" is said on your in-breath and "I'm here" on your out-breath.

As you breathe in saying, "As Is", it reminds you of the willingness to allow yourself to be exactly as you are in this moment. It is the art of letting go of struggling with whatever is (your usual mode), so you can move into the place of healing that comes from allowing yourself to be exactly as you are. If you open to the depth of what "As is" is inviting you into, your belly will soften and your mind will become very curious about what is happening inside of you.

As you say "I'm here" on your out-breath, it reminds you to be with whatever Life is offering you in this moment. It is the willingness to be keenly attentive to what is, in a way that invites your heart to be with the parts of you that are asking to be seen. Remember, attention heals! The parts of you that keep on taking you away from the circle of your breath need somebody to be with them just like a child does, so they can let go. Just imagine how it feels when you are hurting and somebody says, "I am here with you. Tell me about it." Then you will know the healing power of "I'm here".

When you put these two statements together, saying "As Is" on the in-breath and "I'm here" on the out-breath, it reminds you of the healing power of your heart. It is an invitation beyond the endless struggle of trying to be what you think you should be. It is the willingness to embrace all the parts of your being so you can receive the nourishment of the compassionate attention you are hungry for from the only source that really matters, yourself. As you soften around your experience, allowing it to be here and even welcoming it, it will, in its own time, open up and the energy that was bound up in it will expand and release.

After you read the following section, put the book down, close your eyes and begin exploring. If timing your session, add one minute, taking it to ten minutes. If time is not an issue, stay with each step as long as your curiosity is engaged.

Let's begin:

- Close your eyes and dip the finger of your attention into the river of your experience, noticing what it is like to be you right now.

- For at least three in-breaths, tighten your muscles and then very slowly relax everything on your out-breath as you say the great sound of letting go, "Ahh!"

- Bring your attention to the circle of your breath, saying the calming/focusing words, "In...Out; Deep...Slow; Calm...Ease."

Now add "As Is" on the in-breath and "I'm here" on the out-breath to the calming/focusing words (or you can say "As is...I'm here" on its own for this session). Allow yourself to feel the kind of relationship with yourself that these words are pointing to. When you notice a story, a sensation or a feeling that is capturing your attention, taking you away from the circle of your breath, allow "As is…I'm here" to remind you to be open to the experience. Be as welcoming as you can about whatever is arising and then return to your breath, allowing the calming/focusing words to remind you to be with yourself in an attentive and spacious way.

Stay with this as long as it interests you, grounding with your breath and the calming/focusing words, watching things grab your attention and, instead of getting lost in them, giving them the power of your own accepting attention, then returning to the circle of your breath.

- At the end, expand your awareness and be curious about your experience after having given yourself the healing of your own attention.

- When you are ready, open your eyes.

Abbreviated Version:

- Close your eyes and check in, noticing what it is like to be you right now.

- For at least three in-breaths, tighten your muscles and then very slowly relax everything on your out-breath as you say the great sound of letting go, "Ahh!"

- Bring your attention to the circle of your breath, saying the calming/focusing words, "In…Out; Deep…Slow; Calm…Ease; As is…I'm here." (Or you can say "As is…I'm here" by itself)

- If you notice a story, sensation or feeling that is capturing your attention, taking you away from the circle of your breath, allow the essence of "As is…I'm here" to remind you to meet it in an open and spacious way. Then bring your attention back to the circle of your breath and the calming/focusing words.

- At the end, expand your awareness and be curious about your experience after having given yourself the healing of your own attention.

- When you are ready, open your eyes.

Re-memberings

- Life is set up to bring up what has been bound up so it can open up to be freed up so you can show up for Life!

- This is about showing up for your life rather than always trying to make it be what you think it should be.

- Whenever you are identified with the spells that make up your storyteller, you tighten. Your body, heart and mind tighten, dimming the free flowing aliveness that you are.

- Become a tightness detective. Instead of being upset about being upset, become curious.

- When triggered, most people react, blame, fix or run away, which never heals anything. The *you-turn* is about bringing your attention back to you so that you can recognize the stories/sensations/feelings that are asking for the attention they need to let go.

- Every single feeling you have is expressed in your body in a particular way, and your body will signal you long before your mind will that you are reacting to something.

- Ask yourself, "Do I really want my reactions running my life?"

- To experience directly what you are experiencing, know that resistance will be a part of it. You have spent most of your life resisting what you are experiencing.

- By not tightening around discomfort you allow the cloud bank of struggle to pass through you.

- Your discomforts are not here because something is wrong. They are here as your guide through the cloud bank of struggle and back into the meadow of Life.

- Now is the time to stop fighting with the difficulties and discomforts of your life and to learn how to explore them, understanding that discomfort is a doorway.

- "Do I prefer to grow up and relate to Life directly, or do I choose to live and die in fear?"

CHAPTER 7

All is Welcome Here

In the last two chapters we have been developing the muscle of your attention so you could become curious about whatever you are experiencing right now. Through curiosity, you can learn to unhook from many of your spells and allow them simply to pass through you. But the more you turn your attention within, the more you will see that there are some very tightly held parts of you that won't let go when you bring your attention to them. You also need to listen to them and to listen from your heart.

Many of us are afraid to do this, for when we listen, what we hear is often disturbing and confusing. And yet to be fully open to Life, we need to be open to whatever is going on inside of us. There is a whole host of characters within you (e.g. arrogance, despair, righteousness, helplessness, judgment, entitlement, revenge, self-pity, etc.) that you don't want anybody else to know is there. There is no need to be ashamed of these characters, everybody has them. When they don't let go under the light of your curiosity, they need to be listened to. When they are heard, they cease to have power over you.

It is your heart that can approach them, listen to their view of the world, and thus release them from the prison of your resistance to them. When I talk about the heart, I am talking about the energy center in your chest that is open to Life. Whereas your mind is dualistic in nature, caught up most of the time in liking/disliking and wanting/resisting, the energy in your chest is a lover of what is. It includes rather than excludes. It accepts rather than rejects. Your heart trusts rather than fears, and it weaves every single part of you and every single part of your life back into the whole that it truly is.

When you were young, your heart center was open. Life was something you felt from your heart rather than something you thought about. Rather than needing to control and resist, life was magical, fascinating and full of adventure. But you had to shut down your heart. It wasn't safe to keep it open for it was bruised and hurt by events and people in your life. So you retreated into your head and locked the innocence and healing power of your heart deep inside of you. This takes most of the joy out of Life, and whether you recognize it or not, your deepest longing is to live from your heart again. Your deepest longing is to be open to Life, and it is in discovering (un-covering) your heart again that this becomes possible.

-Ω- Let's experience the difference between living from your mind and living from your heart. Take a moment and imagine that sitting in front of you is somebody you deeply love (living or dead, person or animal). Remember a time when your heart was completely open to them and allow your whole being to feel this. If you watch carefully you will see the energy in your chest shifts; it will expand, open and even glow. If you stay with it long enough you will experience your whole body glowing.

Now imagine a time when you reacted to them, maybe becoming afraid of losing their love or being angry about something they had done. Look and you will see that just imagining this closes the openness in your chest, contracting the rest of your body as your mind becomes tight and reactive. This is what happens when your heart becomes closed again.

Which one feels better: the closed, reactive place or the open and loving place? Of course it is the second, for that is who you truly are: an open heart. That place of openness whose source is in your chest is the doorway back into the meadow of Life that is always with you. When it is freed up from the cloud bank of fear, it becomes vibrantly alive, guiding you every step of the way down the path of Life.

The amazingly wonderful thing is that the storyteller in your head, with all of its fears, judgments, resistances, doubts, confusions, shame and addiction to control, is here to teach you about living from your heart again. The full transformation of the spells that make up your cloud bank happens when they are met with your compassionate attention. It is your mind that tries to solve things. It is your heart that dissolves them.

Remember, we have explored throughout this book that the healing you're ready for doesn't come from changing anything. It comes from the ability to *see* and *be with* what is right now. When you are caught in your mind, you try to fix, change and get away from whatever you are experiencing. When your heart begins to open again, you discover the healing of not resisting what you are experiencing. This brings you to the phenomenal healing power of *All is Welcome Here*, which is the opposite of resisting. What you resist you empower, but when you welcome your immediate experience, especially when you stay open around what has been closed inside of you, your spells lose their power over you.

-Ω- Take a moment to wake up your heart center by repeatedly tapping your chest and smiling.

Touching Yourself with Your Own Heart:

At times you may be able to give your close friends and loved ones the spaciousness of your heart, but you, like most people, are probably unskilled at giving this amazing nourishment to yourself. Instead, you have been conditioned to fix, judge, ignore, deny or try to understand what you are experiencing, which is the ultimate seduction, and all of this keeps you caught in your head.

If you stop and truly listen to what you are experiencing in any given moment, you will see that you have a community inside, made up of a cast of characters that have been with you since you were young. (Carl Jung first presented the idea that each one of us is made up of a community of parts.) And if you were honest with yourself, you would see that there are many parts of you that you have locked out of your own heart.

You were conditioned to believe that if you ignored them, keeping them stuffed inside of you through staying very busy, watching TV, eating, drinking, shopping or texting, that they would go away. The startling thing to realize is that when you ignore these parts, they influence you from underneath your everyday awareness, which is much like having young children in charge of your life. (Just think about the last argument you were caught in and you can see how young these parts are.)

To know the aliveness that you long for, every part of you needs to be woven back into your heart. The deep fears, angers, self-judgments and despairs that are hidden inside of you have been with you since you were little, and just like you, they want to be seen, acknowledged, understood and loved so they can let go.

Why is it so powerful to be curious and accepting about what you are experiencing rather than trying to change it in any way? Attention that is accepting heals! One of the most powerful paradoxes you will come across on your healing journey is that true transformation can only happen in an atmosphere of acceptance and listening. When you give accepting attention to whatever you are experiencing, the energy that was bound up in it begins to expand, move, and eventually let go.

To get the sense of what I'm talking about here, imagine having a bad day and sharing it with a friend who, instead of listening to you, tries to fix you, judges you or ignores you. What feelings does that bring up? They're probably not very pleasant. Now imagine that your friend really listens to you from his or her heart, and rather than judging or trying to fix you, your friend accepts you. The chances are you would feel a lot lighter after being listened to in this way because you were given the spaciousness to experience what you were experiencing.

A wonderful example of bringing this kind of listening to ourselves comes from a young woman with whom I have been meeting with for a while. This is her story of touching her experience with her own heart:

> My boyfriend and I had gone downtown to meet up with some friends. After a few hours I got hungry and wanted to go home to make dinner. Sensing that he wanted to stay out longer, I hesitatingly asked if he wanted to come home and eat with me or hang out for a while. He told me he wanted to hang out longer but he would give me a ride home. As we walked to the car I could feel it all building up--the voices in my head started their familiar banter of "I'm not fun enough", "What's wrong with me", and "I don't deserve him". My stomach tightened into a fist. My throat grew into a hard ball of mucus and the space around my heart began to close. All this build-up was so familiar that it carried with it a false sense of security and comfort. It carried with it a spell that had been cast long ago.

> As we drove home, I started to notice something shift in me. I not only realized, but really saw that I was the one watching

this story unfold. I was not the story itself. I could feel the story holding on as if its life depended on it. It did not want to let go. And then I recalled something I had read earlier that week about the power of shifting your perspective when the spells arise. I began to thank all the voices, all the intense energy within, and instead of resisting, I smiled at them, being grateful that they were coming up. I felt my heart open and release as my perspective shifted. I kept repeating to myself, "I allow my heart to be open; I allow all of this to move through my open heart."

It was incredible! My body started to soften, my mind calmed down, and for the rest of the ride home we laughed and smiled and expressed our deep love for one another. It was a revelation for me. By opening my heart to this experience, I was able to see it for what it was: a spell that wanted to be healed; a spell that needed my attention; a spell that deserved compassion and kindness; a spell that showed up to open me to the love and healing power within.

-Ω- For a few minutes breathe in and out of your heart. Then ride the waves of your breath, saying silently to yourself, "As is…I'm here." Meet yourself exactly as you are.

Everything Longs for the Heart:

Why have you not fully met yourself with your own heart? Because you were trained (by your parents, teachers, peers and society) to believe that you aren't okay the way you are and need to be fixed. Fixing is just the endless game of your storyteller and comes from being taught to judge and fear what goes on inside of you. Remember, there is nothing inside to be ashamed of or afraid of. These beliefs were just conditioned into you, and when you finally look at them, they are no more substantial than a cloud. Also, we're all nutty as fruitcakes, so the parts you have hidden deep inside because of fear and shame – everybody else has, too!

Instead of seeing yourself as somebody who has unacceptable parts that need to be fixed (and thus a victim to your life), we are turning that around 180 degrees into the truth that nothing needs to be fixed; you just need the power of an aware heart. In order to access the full power of your own heart, it helps to recognize that your wounded parts have been given to you by Life to teach you about the power of accepting attention. You don't have these parts because your parents screwed you up or because God fell asleep on the job. There is nobody to blame. Your parents (teachers, siblings and peers) were just the delivery system of the wounds that you took on that are here to teach you about opening your heart.

Rather than being a victim to these so-called unacceptable parts of yourself, you begin to see that the spells you took on when you were very young are the doorway back into the meadow. They are the raw material of your awakening, and when you resist them, your cloud bank only gets denser. When you bring them home to your heart, your cloud bank thins and the meadow of joy and aliveness that is Life makes itself known again. For in the long run, the only thing that truly heals is love, and Life will put you in the situations you need to bring up the parts that need the healing of your heart.

There is a woman in one of my groups who was unknowingly and deeply betrayed by her boyfriend right before they broke up. A month after the breakup, he told her he just tested positive for HIV. She came to group a few hours after he told her and a few hours before she herself was tested. Words cannot describe how amazing that group was - human beings opening to what was showing up inside all of us and meeting it all in our hearts. Later that afternoon, her first test came back negative, but she has two more to go. In the middle of this, she emailed this to all of us in the group and gave me permission to share it with all of you:

> I wanted to tell you again how grateful I am for your love and for how preciously you have been holding the space for me in this cracking open that Life is giving me. I continue to be amazed at how I am showing up for this process, and how much is being revealed and delighted within me through opening to this experience. I fully understand what Mary means when she says there is no part of myself that does not deserve my loving attention, and there is nothing worth closing around.
>
> This doesn't mean there haven't been waves of grief, sadness, anger and terror, but they have passed through quickly as I've

softened into them and allowed them the space to be here. Last night resistance showed up, and I spent the hours from 10pm-3am working with it, not closing it out of my heart.

When I was in resistance, the picture of being in an inflatable raft in full body armor on a raging river with huge rocks jutting out from every angle came to me. When I resist what I'm experiencing, I desperately try to stay clear of the rocks, fighting a losing battle as water capsizes my boat and it begins to deflate. Not a fun or enjoyable experience. But, when I open my heart and allow whatever I am experiencing to be as it is, it is as if I am in that raft, in my swimsuit, lounging and soaking up the sun, delighting in the waves and the turns, and feeling the exhilaration of the river carrying me safely on my way.

What a difference a small shift in my thinking makes from resistance to: 'I am right where I need to be,' 'Life is supporting me,' 'I am being carried down this river,' and 'I can let go and trust that I am safe.' I wanted to share this with you all because there are so many smaller challenges that I once thought it impossible to turn towards. Now I know without a doubt that if I can do this with the possibility of HIV and everything else that goes with this challenge, there is not one thing that I cannot hold in my heart and eventually love. I know this to be true for all of you as well, and so I am holding this space for you in whatever is showing up in your life today.

What would it be like to realize that all your painful feelings are just frozen energy that is asking for love? What would your life look like if you realized that the energy that is bound up inside of you truly will thaw when touched by full acceptance? Most of the time, you just want your spells and the discomfort that they generate to go away. What your feelings want is your heart, and they will keep on showing up until they receive the lasting healing of your accepting attention.

-Ω- Take a moment and gently rest a hand on your chest. Feel your heart beating and your breath rising and falling. Can you allow yourself to be exactly where you are right now? Can you give yourself a smile?

I See You:

We are now ready to give our spells the accepting attention they need in order to let go. Before we do this it is important to remember two core truths we have been exploring throughout the book. The first is that your pain is made worse by your resistance to it. In fact, your resistance turns your pain into suffering. This is true for physical, mental and emotional pain. What a joy it is to discover that when you stop resisting what you are experiencing and touch it with your heart, it not only becomes more bearable, but it also has a tendency to pass through you much more quickly.

The second truth is that the spells you have bought into your whole life are not you. They are just conditioned states that keep you separate from the meadow of your being. They can be seen and seen through. And they aren't even yours: they are ours, for all human beings take on these spells. It is a wonderful moment when, caught in a spell, you recognize that other people, right at that exact time, are lost in that story, too!

These two truths will help you develop your capacity to turn toward your experience. As you do, you will be able to see that the spells of your cloud bank show up as stories in your head that generate sensations and feelings in your body.

Let's take anger for example. It may show up as a tight fist around your stomach. If you look carefully, you will see the story that generates that fist. It may be saying, "They did it wrong" or "I am going to make them pay." It also has an emotional component and the feeling of anger is energetically different than any other feeling. Whether you notice the reactions of your cloud bank as they express in your body, how they talk in your head, or how they feel, every moment of *knowticing* makes a difference.

There is a very simple but profound way to bring the power of accepting attention to what you are experiencing. It is through saying "I see you" to whatever you are noticing. This allows you to access the healing power of the 'you-turn'. In saying "I see you," your attention and your immediate experience come closer together. It opens the possibility that the holding you are noticing can begin to soften with the help of your *knowticing*. You may find that, for some parts that were frozen at a very early age, saying "I see you" is too much for them. They may be too scared to come out of hiding even though they really want to be seen. If so, try saying, "I acknowledge that you are here."

Every moment of saying "I see you" is a moment of consciousness. Over time as you develop the muscle of your curiosity enough, you will be able to bring the healing of compassionate curiosity to whatever is happening in your life. Then you will be able to see that your old reactions want to be released. They want to be able simply to pass through you without you getting caught in their stories.

The draw to get caught in the reactions of your cloud bank is very strong. A good example comes from a friendship of mine. After awhile I noticed that the only time we connected was when I called. Then there came a time when he wouldn't return my calls. I reached him one day and asked how he was doing and he said he was fine, but busy. I then shared with him the feelings that came up inside of me when he didn't return my calls. He said he understood, but he still didn't respond to my calls. I finally stopped calling, but when I thought of him I would oftentimes feel anger.

It was very seductive to stay with my anger, but I was awake enough to know this was an opportunity to be with some bound up energy inside of me. When I thought of him, I initially felt either anger (and thought, "He is wrong.") or self-judgment (and thought, "What did I do wrong?") which is just anger turned within. I would then turn my attention to where the anger/self-judgment was expressing itself in my body and give it my attention, letting it know "I see you."

As I met the anger, it would step aside and reveal a deep sadness in my belly. I could see how young it was and how this was a core experience of my childhood. (My father, with whom I lived for the first 12 years of my life, completely ignored me because I was not the boy he had wanted.) I could also see how much of my life was about trying to get away from this painful feeling of not mattering that had gotten frozen in my belly. Finally, this feeling was mattering to me, and I was giving it the recognition it needed in order for it to let go.

-Ω- What's happening in your belly right now?

So through this friendship, Life was *setting me up* to *bring up* this *bound up* feeling of despair in my belly that I had buried there long ago. Rather than staying caught in the story of anger/despair, I turned toward my experience and, through the power of telling it, "I see you," it opened up under the light of my accepting attention. (Remember, this is just frozen energy that longs to be released.) Because I was no longer holding it inside of me through my resistance to it, it was freed up to move right on through me. That is the power of attention!

Through meeting it, I realize how much this feeling of not mattering has influenced my life, putting a wall between me and Life. Now that I can be present with it, I am much more able to show up fully for Life. Before, when this feeling was triggered, I would be silently angry at people for not being with me the way I wanted them to be. Then I would withdraw because it brought up this old pain. Now that I am no longer afraid of this feeling, it is much easier to accept people as they are,. If it looks to me as though someone is ignoring me or rejecting me, I do the *you-turn* and acknowledge what this brings up inside of me instead of projecting the responsibility for my feeling onto them.

All the deep feelings inside of us are just energy that got trapped in spells and bound up in our bodies. And like all energy, they want to move. They want to be set free. When you find yourself in a situation where your old reactions surface, you can help them to move through you by taking a walk, enjoying a shower, or talking to a friend. But that just temporarily moves them. What they need to be set free is your accepting attention. Now I am grateful when an old feeling rises to the surface so I can give it the attention it needs simply to pass through me.

To awaken, it is important to know that there is no such thing as an ordinary moment. There are only two kinds of moments happening in your life: Life is either inviting you to be fully open to Life right here, right now, or it is putting you in the situations that are needed to *bring up* what has been *bound up* inside of you so it can *open up* to be *freed up*.

At the beginning, you may only be able to notice that you are struggling. You can then say to yourself, "I see that I am getting tight. There is something inside of me that is asking for my attention." That may not seem like a lot, but it is a moment of consciousness. You can also ask for clarity from the wisdom that is always with you by asking, "What is asking to be seen?" We explored this in depth in Chapter Four, discovering that to ask for clarity signals Life that you want to see what is asking to be transformed. You then let that request go to work its magic from underneath your everyday awareness.

It does take courage to turn toward yourself, giving the bound up energy inside of you the attention it needs to let go. To discover this courage, ask yourself, "Do I really want this stuff running my life?" You are only alive for a very short time, and I can assure you, at the end of your life you won't be celebrating all of the times you got hooked into reaction, falling into your anger, fear, sadness or shame. Instead you will be oh so grateful for developing the ability to unhook from these energy patterns so that your reactions can simply pass through you, leaving you in touch with the meadow of Life.

-Ω- Take a moment now and dip the finger of your attention into the river of experience that is your body. Whatever you notice – maybe a slight headache, contentment in your belly, tightness in your solar plexus, your feet are warm – let your attention settle there, becoming curious about how the energy is expressing itself in that area. To whatever you notice, say, "I see you".

What It Is Like to Listen:

We have already explored that many of these spells will simply pass through you when you can see them for what they are: conditioning you took on when you were very young. Let us now begin to explore how to stand with the spells that are so deeply embedded inside of you that they need more than just being seen. They need to be listened to also. As they receive your focused, compassionate listening, these spells that have influenced you your whole life will let go and you will experience again the meadow of your being that is always with you, right here, right now.

A quote from author Geneen Roth, speaks directly to this when she says: "Most of our suffering comes from resisting what is already here, particularly our feelings. All any feeling wants is to be welcomed, touched, allowed. It wants attention. It wants kindness. If you treated your feelings with as much love as you treated your dog or your cat or your child, you'd feel as if you were living in heaven every day of your sweet life."

The best way to describe what Geneen is talking about is with an experience I had at my chiropractor's office. To understand the depth of the old spells that were awakened inside of me that day, you need to know that a big part of how my storyteller was put together was from a sense that I didn't matter, i.e., my needs are not important and I don't have a right even to voice them. For most of my childhood I lived in the same bedroom with an older sister whose survival system was all about being the best. She saw me as less than, a bother, and she made sure I got the message that she was best at everything. There was no one in my world to give me acceptance and affirmation, so this created deep spells inside of me, and a couple of the core ones were triggered at the chiropractor's office.

That morning I woke up not feeling well after dealing with an intestinal bug for a few days, but I still needed to see my chiropractor. I usually set aside 30 minutes for the appointment, but regularly I am in and out in about 10 minutes. This morning I had already been waiting for 20 minutes when a new person checked in and sat down in the waiting room with me. Five minutes later, he was taken back to see the doctor. When I asked the receptionist why he went back before me, she said she was going to go and check on it and didn't come back for what seemed like a very long time. When she did she said, "Yes, we made a mistake." When I responded that I had now been waiting for half an hour and I was on a tight time frame, she said she couldn't do anything about it.

I sat down and immediately what arose inside of me was a lot of anger from the "I must control Life" spell. Life wasn't doing what I wanted it to do so my storyteller was angry! It is important to know that when spells get awakened like mine was that morning, our reaction is usually irrational in relationship to what is going on right now. But it is not irrational in relationship to how it was frozen inside of us when we were young. So when they get triggered, they show up exactly as they were in our youth. That is why we can have such over-the-top reactions to seemingly inconsequential things.

I was having an over-the-top reaction. My heart was pounding and I had a knot in my stomach. The stories that were raging through my mind were very young: "This is not fair." "It was my turn." "I will tell their boss what they did." "They need to be told they were wrong." "I will just get up and leave and show them."

It felt like 99.999% of me wanted to run with my reaction because this experience was super fuel for the reactive righteousness that permeates the "I must control Life" spell. On one level it felt good to be *right* and my storyteller wanted to prove that I had been wronged (a sub spell of "I must do it right"). But I am awake enough to know that to give these thoughts energy would only engender more suffering and I would miss an opportunity to heal some young and wounded parts of myself. Rather than being *right*, I want to be *free*.

So the first thing I did was to allow a deep breath of letting go and then to acknowledge that I was caught. This may not seem like such a big step, but it is. For most people, when Life brings one of their spells up to the surface, they simply slip into its story and react from that place, bringing more suffering into their lives. Seeing how tight I had become permitted me to recognize that I was caught in a spell and this allowed me to take a step back from what I was experiencing.

I then asked Life for clarity. This is what we explored in Chapter Four: learning how to see that there is an Intelligence that is greater than you that is always with you. It is also seeing that, embedded in every challenge Life gives you, is a piece of your puzzle, but you don't need to figure this all out on your own. You can turn it over to Life. So I asked, "What is asking to be met here?"

I then did the *you-turn*, turning my attention toward my immediate experience. I first went to my body, noticing my stomach was in knots. As I allowed my attention to settle there I could feel the feeling of anger radiating like a hot stove from my stomach. I said, "I see you." But this was such a strong reaction in me that it didn't simply dissipate under the light of my attention. Instead, it needed the attention of my heart. I then said, "It is okay that you are here." (The core parts of our storyteller need to hear this.)

Then I was willing to listen. In learning how to listen to whatever is coming up inside of you, you will discover that each part has its own particular view of the world and they all respond to being listened to just as you do when you are upset. So I asked this angry one, "Tell me about your world," and simply listened as it told me its story. It raged, blamed, justified, and defended the right to be a victim. I didn't judge it or ignore what it was saying. Instead I let it know I was here with it and I understood.

I was then able to let it know that it wouldn't be helpful to strike out in anger, since that reaction only brings forth more reaction. I also reminded it of all the times in my life that I was able to move out of reaction into responding and how much healing came from that.

Under the light of my accepting attention, the angry one calmed down and let go. I was then able to see the underlying vulnerability that the anger was trying to protect – the feeling that "I don't matter" that is part of the "I am unlovable" spell. I also asked about its view of the world. As it spoke, there was so much sadness, along with the belief that this happened because she was bad (a sub spell of the "I am wrong" spell).

It may sound irrational that there was sadness about having my turn taken, but remember, our reactions to unsettling experiences in our life are rarely about what is going on right now. They come from the spells we took on when we were little and they have been waiting our whole life to be given the attention they need from us to heal. This feeling of not mattering was one of the core spells I took on, so rather than judging or trying to stop what was going on inside of me, I listened.

When this deep grief felt heard, I was able to say, "You are not alone any more. I have grown up and I can be with you in the way you needed somebody to be with you when you were young. I'm here now. This didn't happen because you are bad. This happened so you would come close enough to the surface of my awareness and I could meet you with my heart." My whole body began to glow in joy for in that moment the feeling of not mattering truly mattered to me!

The anger had completely dissipated simply by being heard. The grief calmed down, but a bit of it stayed with me for most of the day, giving me the opportunity to keep meeting it with my heart with "I see you. I'm here."

-Ω- Pause for a moment and turn your attention toward yourself. Whatever you notice (cold feet, a feeling of joy, an anxious mind, etc.), say, "I see you. I'm here."

In the beginning of this experience my heart was closed, closed to the receptionist and closed to myself. As I was able to turn toward my experience and give it the light of my attention, I began to soften inside and my heart began to open. I could feel how young each of these parts were, both the angry one that was trying to protect and the more vulnerable one that felt it didn't matter. I could also see that what both of these were asking for was the same thing I ask for: not to be judged or fixed or ignored, but instead to be seen, heard, and allowed to have their experience. As they felt heard, they let go!

The experience in the chiropractor's office was the culmination of a lifetime of running away from the deep pain of not mattering and then learning how to turn toward it. The pain of this spell was so great I literally had to bury it when I was young in order to survive. That didn't make it go away. In fact, I became extremely compulsive, all in an attempt to run away from this feeling. This spell has also influenced many of the decisions of my life without my ever being aware of it.

It took me years to discover this pathway from the reactive mind to the listening and accepting heart. In the beginning not much seemed to happen, for I didn't yet understand the power of just one moment of having my attention and my immediate experience together. But slowly, as I became willing to be honest with myself about what I was experiencing, for a moment here and a moment there, I began to be able to see and listen to the parts of myself that I had hated and feared. I could notice that when somebody said something that triggered me, instead of defending myself or making them wrong, I would be curious about my reaction.

I then learned how to be curious about the tightness in my body that the feelings were generating. Maybe there was a lump in my throat that was the tip of an iceberg of grief or a tight fist in my stomach that signaled the hidden anger of a lifetime. At the beginning I could only notice what was going on in my body for a moment or two before the urge to turn away took over or the sensation seemed to go away. But in those moments I learned how to say, "I see you and I want to get to know you," without needing anything to happen.

Slowly my spells found the courage to reveal themselves to me. As I let my attention settle into the holdings in my body, these parts would let me see how they experienced the world. I could feel what they were feeling and I could hear their story. Because they so deeply longed for the light of my accepting attention, they would eventually find the courage to show themselves fully to me. Now all of my parts are enfolded in my heart.

-Ω- Soften your belly and say to yourself, "All is welcome here." Notice what happens inside of you when you say that. Does the mind resist it, tightening you? Or does it soften your experience, allowing your heart a voice? Or maybe there is a little bit of both.

Deepening your Listening:

I used to teach a particular pathway for meeting spells with your heart. But, I saw many people's storytellers take this over and try to do this meeting, which only led to frustration. Now I invite people to recognize that the spells inside of them long for exactly what everybody longs for when they want somebody to be there for them - compassionate listening. With that understanding, it will be easier for you to find your own pathway for being present for your spells.

With that said, it can be helpful to recognize the basic pathway for healing your spells through the light of your attention and you can see it in my experience at the chiropractor's office. First of all, I **recognized** that I was upset. Then I **asked Life for clarity.** My attention was then naturally drawn toward my immediate experience and I **became curious** about what was here. I then **acknowledged what I was experiencing** through saying, "I see you." We have explored the compassionate curiosity of "I see you" all throughout the book and many of your spells will let go when met in this way.

But the spells that we are most afraid of or ashamed of are the ones that need another step. They need you to **listen to their world**. Remember that when you are having a bad day, this is what you want, too. This is where you say to whatever you are noticing, "I want to hear about your world."

For many of our deeply frozen spells it is very important to say, "*When you are ready*, I want to hear about your world." Because we have judged them, resisted them, and constantly tried to get rid of them, it takes them a while to trust that we truly want to hear about their world. They are like shy baby deer who will hide when we try to find them. But they truly want connection, and with patience, they will come out of hiding and let you see them.

Each of your spells has a particular view of the world. They are made up of stories that were created when you were young, and they respond to being heard just like you do. If you are willing to listen, they will tell you about their experience of the world. Your job is to listen, for this is about giving these parts a voice for that is what allows the blocked energy to move.

There is no need to be ashamed or afraid of what any part tells you. Remember, these parts were frozen inside of you when you were young, so they have the view of a child. They have waited their whole life finally to be heard so they can let go under the gaze of your accepting attention. Whether what is asking to be met inside of you shows up as sensations, feelings or stories, they all just want to be heard.

-Ω- Bring your attention to a familiar place of holding in your body and say to it, "I want to hear how you experience the world." It doesn't matter if anything happens here. Just the willingness to let it know you want to know matters. When it feels safe enough, it will reveal itself to you.

For many of your parts, when they are heard, they will calm down, revealing inside of you the vast space of peace that you really are. But your deepest spells may need the final gift I gave to myself in the chiropractor's office. It is what I call **the Invitation**. This is where you invite the spell into a perspective that is different from what it has held its whole life. This is what I did with both the angry one and the one that felt it didn't matter. A part that feels it is unlovable may need to hear that you accept it as it is. The part that feels all alone may need to hear that you are here with it, and though at times you may leave, you will come back as soon as you can.

One of the most poignant moments in my awakening came as I was working with the part of me that felt that I was bad and wrong to my core. After listening to it, I could see that it needed to hear a different view. So I said, "We have turned out to be a good person." This part was stunned by this news. It said, "Really?" It had been frozen for so long in the belief that I was bad that it started to cry for the sheer relief of it. It kept on saying, "Is this really true?" And when I would respond, "Yes," a fresh wave of tears would come.

Writing down what a spell says can help you to see the world of your spells. Rather than writing paragraphs, I find it is best to write down one-liners. Ask a part how it sees Life and, I assure you, it will be very revealing. My life truly began to open up when I was able to listen to the part inside of me that felt I was a bad person. I had spent most of my life secretly believing this, but also trying to deny it. As I wrote down how this part viewed me, I could see that its perceptions were very young and were truly irrational. There were even a few beliefs that this part still wanted to defend as true, such as, "You did this when you were 23 and that proves you are bad." This part believed that if I wasn't perfect, then I was bad! But there is no such thing as a perfect person!

Know that only the deepest of spells need this kind of listening and the offer of a different perception. It may take a while before these spells will be able to share with you their view of the world. It takes time to create the kind of relationship that allows them to feel safe enough to be real with you about their world. Also, it is only after they are truly listened to that they will be open to a different view. And just as you calm down and feel much lighter when you are heard, your deep listening allows these very young and hidden parts of you to let go enough for the energy that was bound up in them to be freed!

Finding Your Pathway:

It is a truly healing moment in your life when you recognize that these spells are not who you are. You are that which can see them and give them the accepting attention that they need in order to let go. As you become more familiar with your spells, it is startling to recognize that they have never been allowed to have their experience. You are so trained to turn away from them that they have never felt heard. I assure you, the joy that comes when you truly recognize and listen to a part of yourself that you have denied, fallen into or run away from your whole life is delicious!

It is also delicious to finally recognize that it is okay to be experiencing whatever you are experiencing! To discover how to meet ourselves exactly as we are brings forth such joy. We have been waiting a long time to heal the spell that it is not okay to authentically be ourselves. It takes time to learn this because we have been conditioned to turn away from what we are experiencing rather than toward it. Patience is key in this kind of healing. It is like learning a new language: the language of the heart. Your heart carries an energy of healing that is beyond any fixing, changing or resisting that your mind can do. Your heart is all about non-judgment, inclusion, allowing, willingness to listen, and acceptance.

There is a wonderful thing you can do with your imagination to help you see what your spells are asking of you so you can discover your own pathway from your reactive mind to your attentive heart. Imagine coming into a large room that seems to be empty. Suddenly a movement in the corner captures your attention. As you walk toward this corner, you see it is a frightened little child who is trying to hide. In a flash, you know this child is feeling exactly what you have been feeling. What would you say? How would you be with this child? Whatever response you have is exactly what your feelings want from you. Then turn your attention toward yourself and be with yourself in the exact way you were with this child.

If this doesn't call to you, you can also imagine what you would have liked your parents to say to you and how you would have liked them to be with you. You can also imagine this with your mate or your friends. Right here, in your imagination, is what you need from yourself.

There are two other wonderful practices you can add to your life, as well. The first one is, whenever you find yourself caught in struggle, bring your hand to the area of your body that is tightening. If you are angry, it may be a fist in your stomach. If you are sad, it could be a lump in your throat. Gently lay your hand there, and as you bring your full attention to that area say, "I see you. It is okay that you are here." Remember, you are not trying to make anything happen. Just a moment or two of bringing your full attention to your immediate experience makes a difference in the long run.

The second one is, if you are not clear about what is reacting inside of you, you can bring your hand to your heart and either pat or circle it around your chest and say, "I accept myself as I am." Remember, when you recognize that the meadow of your being IS Love, you finally know that there is not a part of you that doesn't deserve to be included in the meadow of your heart. Then you realize that no matter what Life brings up inside of you, all is welcome here.

So the question is, how do you want to live? Do you want to live from your mind that keeps you lost in a storyteller that reacts and controls or from your heart that opens you to Life? For most of us, that choice is becoming very clear. We want to move beyond our addiction to struggle and meet ourselves and our lives with the healing of our hearts.

RE-MEMBERING SECTION

Re-membering Session

Each week we have been deepening your ability to bring your attention and your immediate experience together. It is now time to discover that you can relate directly to whatever you are experiencing rather than being lost in it or running away from it.

This week, as you are riding the waves of your breath, when your storyteller and the feelings and sensations that it generates grab your attention, you are invited to be curious about what has grabbed your attention. It may be a story about what happened yesterday, or a pain in your arm, or a feeling of sadness in your chest. Then say, "I see you." to whatever you are noticing and then return to your breath. This allows you to relate to what you are experiencing rather than being identified with it.

"I see you" accesses the phenomenal healing of your heart. It is saying that for this moment I am giving whatever I am noticing my full accepting attention. You will have time in the next session where you can actually explore what is taking you away. For now, see it, acknowledge it by saying, "I see you," and then return to your breath and the calming/focusing words. Remember, these are all just expressions of the cloud bank and the invitation is to acknowledge them, let them go and come back to the sanctuary of your breath.

Some days you will easily see what has captured your attention and effortlessly return to the ground of your breath. Other days your storyteller will be very strong and when you come back to your breath, your attention will immediately bounce back into the stories. Know that on those days even one moment of seeing what has taken you away and then bringing your attention back to your breath is a moment of deep healing. It doesn't matter if your attention goes right back into your storyteller and even stays there. Moments of relating to what you are experiencing by saying "I see you," matter!

This is why there is no such thing as a good session or a bad session. Some of the most powerful sessions you will have are when your storyteller is all stirred up and you have just moments where you recognize that your attention is again caught in your mind. In that recognition, you will more and more easily be able to let your stories go, coming back to the sanctuary of your breath.

After you read the following section, put the book down, close your eyes and begin exploring. If timing your session, add one minute, taking it to eleven minutes. If time is not an issue, stay with each step as long as your curiosity is engaged.

Let's begin:

- Close your eyes and check in, noticing what it is like to be you right now.

- For at least three in-breaths, tighten your muscles and then very slowly relax everything on your out-breath as you say the great sound of letting go, "Ahh!"

- Bring your attention to the circle of your breath, saying the calming/focusing words, "In...Out; Deep...Slow; Calm...Ease; As is...I'm here." (Or you can say "As is...I'm here" by itself).

- Whenever you notice that you are no longer fully with your breath, be curious about what your attention has been drawn to. Say to whatever you are noticing, "I see you." or "I see you. I'm here." if that resonates with you.

- If you feel called to do so, you can spend some time exploring what you are noticing through curiosity. If not, simply bring your attention back to your breath and the calming/focusing words. Know that every moment of saying "I see you," and then returning to your breath is a moment of healing.

- At the end, expand your awareness and be curious about your experience of giving yourself the healing of your own attention.

- When you are ready, open your eyes.

Abbreviated Version:

- Close your eyes and check in, noticing what it is like to be you right now.

- For at least three in-breaths, tighten your muscles and then very slowly relax everything on your out-breath as you say the great sound of letting go, "Ahh!"

- Bring your attention to the circle of your breath, saying the calming/focusing words.

- Whenever you notice that you are no longer fully with your breath, be curious about what your attention has been drawn to.

- Whatever you notice, say "I see you," and then bring your attention back to your breath and the calming/focusing words.

- At the end, expand your awareness and be curious about your experience after having given yourself the healing of your own attention.

- When you are ready, open your eyes.

Re-memberings

- To be fully open to Life, we need to be open to whatever is going on inside of us.

- There is a whole host of characters within you that you don't want anybody else to know is there. There is no need to be ashamed of these. Everybody has them.

- It is your heart that can approach them, listen to their view of the world, and thus release them from the prison of your resistance to them.

- Your mind is dualistic in nature, liking/disliking, wanting/resisting most all day long. Your heart is the opposite, for it is a lover of what is. It includes rather than excludes. It accepts rather than rejects, and it can weave every single part of you back into the whole that it truly is.

- When you were young, your heart center was open. As you shut it down, you retreated into your mind and locked the innocence and healing power of your heart deep inside of you.

- When your heart begins to open again, you discover the healing of not resisting what you are experiencing. This brings you to the phenomenal healing power of "All is Welcome Here!"

- There is nobody to blame. Your parents (and siblings) were just the delivery system for the wounds you took on that are here to teach you about your heart.

- Transformation happens in an atmosphere of acceptance and listening. When you give accepting attention, the tightly held energy that was bound up inside begins to expand and move.

- You don't need to be fixed. Fixing is the endless game of the storyteller that comes from being taught to judge and fear what goes on inside of you.

- Most of your pain is your resistance to your pain.

- The spells that you have bought into throughout your life are not you. They are just conditioned states that keep you separate from the meadow of your being.

CHAPTER 8

All is Well—Come Here

You are on the journey back to the meadow of your being, discovering how to use your mind to be curious about what is rather than trying to control it. Learning how to turn toward your experience rather than away from it allows you access to the powerful healing force of your own heart. It is through the heart that all of the energy that was tightly held in the spells you took on can now be released. And the more bound up energy you release, the more you show up for Life, rediscovering the meadow of your being where everything flows, everything is alive and everything is Love.

As you are gathering the insight and the willingness to be compassionately attentive to what you are experiencing rather than identifying with it, it is helpful to imagine that you come in three layers:

The top layer is your mind, and instead of using it to be curious about Life, you (like most people) have turned it into a storyteller that narrates your world. Your storyteller is based on fear and glued together with judgment and it talks all day long! Its world is all about controlling you and controlling Life. It likes and dislikes, trying to get to what it wants and getting rid of what it doesn't. When it can't change you and your life in the way it wants, it will oftentimes turn to compulsions to numb you. It is this resistance to your immediate experience, and all of the stories that come out of resistance, that creates the cloud bank which fills your head.

The second layer is made up of all of the so-called unacceptable, unmet parts of yourself. These are the parts that you don't want yourself or anybody else to know about, so the controlling, compulsive top layer buries them deep inside you. They are the youngest, most vulnerable parts of you that are afraid they are not good enough, that they are too much of this and not enough of that, and that Life is not safe. They are so despairing that you feel if you come close to them you would drown. When you keep them buried, they don't go away. Instead, they influence you from underneath your everyday awareness.

The bottom layer is who you really are. It is the meadow of your being. When you live from this place, there is a twinkle in your eye, an aliveness in your body and a vibrancy and radiance in your being. In the meadow you are no longer caught up in *doing* Life. Instead you are *being* Life, reconnecting with your natural trust that allows you to show up for Life rather than being stuck in your head, always trying to make it be what you think it should be. This is the place you lived in when you were very young, until many of the feelings and sensations you were experiencing became too much and you buried them inside (second layer) and retreated to your head (top layer).

On this journey back to yourself, the meadow is the place that opens up when you discover how to use your mind (the top layer) to be curious about what you are experiencing. The meadow reveals itself when you are curious rather than endlessly trying to fix, understand, and generally resist what is going on inside of you, especially the most hidden and unacceptable parts (the second layer). Through the power of curiosity, you can cut through the mind's penchant for resisting your experience and bring to the second layer the accepting attention it needs in order to be healed. The more you meet your immediate experience with an aware heart, the more you discover an amazing truth: every single part of you that you have resisted because you are afraid or ashamed of it contains a doorway into the joy and peace of the meadow (the bottom layer).

-Ω- Take a moment now, and dip the finger of your attention into the river of your experience. The meadow is right here with you. Don't try to find it, just use your mind to notice Life. Fully experience it, right here, right now.

∞

Let us now do a brief overview of what we have explored about who you think you are and who you truly are. The most important truth is that right now, as you are sitting here, you are the meadow. Your body is filled with radiance, your heart is full of love, and there is deep trust in the flow of Life in every cell of your being. All of these generate a spaciousness within you that rests in the vast stillness at the heart of Life.

And yet, most of the time, you don't notice this meadow of your being. Instead, you pay attention to your storyteller that is made up of all sorts of spells you took on when you were young. This storyteller in your head talks all day long, trying to manage Life. In its penchant for management, it doesn't know how to engage with Life right here, right now.

You are being invited to move beyond management into engagement with Life. All is well – come here! It is safe to show up for Life! This is what you long for: the joy of opening to Life and trusting it! Again, remember that trust is not trusting that you will get what you *want*. Trust understands that you will get what you *need* in order to come out of the cloud bank of struggle. Trust trusts both the easy and the difficult aspects of life.

There is a wonderful quote from Erich Fromm, author, philosopher and psychoanalyst, that speaks directly to this: "If one does not know that everything has its time, and wants to force things, then indeed one will never succeed in becoming concentrated – nor in the art of loving."

As you soften into the flow, knowing as it says in the Bible "to everything there is a season," then you become what Fromm calls 'concentrated.' This means showing up for what is here – both the easy and the difficult – discovering that there are no ordinary moments in your life. Life is speaking to you at all times, showing you the spells you took on. The jewel in this quote is that he brings it all together in the statement about the art of loving. He understands that as you discover how to see your spells with love, your cloud bank thins and you discover that this whole journey is about becoming Love!

So you are getting to know your storyteller, not to fix it, change it, or get rid of it, but to discover how to see it for what it is, a storyteller that is based on fear, created in your mind when you were a child and glued together with judgment. The more you can see it, the more your cloud bank can dissipate and the more you can know and live from the meadow of Love again.

Four Tools of Awakening

Let us do a brief synopsis, with examples, of each of the four tools for transforming your storyteller that we have been exploring: curiosity, partnering with your wisdom self, your aware heart, and changing your relationship to discomfort.

Curiosity:

Everything we have explored comes under the umbrella of simply being curious in an accepting way about what you are experiencing. This ability to turn toward your experience rather than getting lost in it or turning away is one of the most healing tools available to a human being. It is powerful because, in a moment of curiosity, you step out of your storyteller. Now you are now relating *to* it rather than *from* it. You don't need to understand exactly what is going on. The simple recognition that you are caught opens a space around your contraction allowing you to see it from a broader perspective.

As your curiosity develops, you will be fascinated with what is going on inside of you, especially when you are triggered by Life. This is the time to say, "I am going to let what is happening inside of me take place." This is about fully experiencing whatever you are experiencing without getting lost in its stories. As you give your experience the fullness of your accepting attention, you can oftentimes feel the energy that was bound up inside of you beginning to move and let go.

Through this ability to see what your storyteller is up to, you will discover more and more how not to resist your experience, even the scary, dark and so called negative parts of you. These are not 'bad' parts that need to be gotten rid of. We are all a mixture of dark and light just like the yin/yang symbol reminds us. And your dark parts are full of richness and gifts that they will reveal to you when they receive the light of your accepting attention.

Thich Naht Hahn, the beloved Buddhist monk and author, speaks to this in his book *The Joy of Full Consciousness* when he says, "The fear, anger and suffering in us are like useful compost. We must not try to throw them out the window. They are quite necessary in order for flowers like compassion, joy and happiness to bloom in us… This is the basis of all our practice. Without it, we will continue to suffer. We will continue to believe that we have to get rid of these negative states in order to be happy. On the contrary, it is very important to accept them."

A woman in one of my groups shared an experience that speaks directly to the power of exploring what you are experiencing in an accepting way, rather than turning it into a problem that needs to be fixed/gotten rid of:

> I was cooking dinner and looking around at my messy house and the thought/spell came into my mind; "I'm tired and overwhelmed." Once I bought into that story, I noticed my energy sink. Then my perception shifted and I realized that *the tired and overwhelmed parts of me are here.* That small shift didn't cause the same energy sink and created more spaciousness. I then said, "The tired and overwhelmed ones are visiting." What a shift that made! It acknowledged that it's all temporary, and this too shall pass. It opened me to even more spaciousness.
>
> I then had some insights about the meadow/cloud bank analogy. The cloud bank of our mind/stories is just like the weather - it comes and goes. Some days it's sunny, some days it's rainy, some days it's snowy, etc. I can't control the weather, and it's not permanent. It's always shifting and impossible to control. The only choice is to experience it as it is – to see it.

Through turning toward her experience, she not only didn't fall into identification with her storyteller, she also discovered the spaciousness that the struggling self is always happening in. In this spaciousness, the energy of tiredness didn't get trapped inside of her through resistance. Instead it simply passed right on through.

It is also helpful in allowing your stories to pass through you to soften your belly and breathe into the experience, for it is in softening around your stories that they let go. It is truly a delight when you discover how much you hold your breath when a spell has taken over and how powerful it is to go in the opposite direction. A deep, open breath moves energy. But rather than trying to take a deep breath (which oftentimes brings more tension because you are *trying* to breathe deeply), you focus on your outbreath and, for as many breaths as it calls to you, you let them be long, slow and deep. This calms your mind and brings an opening around what is trying to close. (You can access a long, slow out-breath through the Candle Breath we explored in Chapter Two's Re-Membering Session.)

-Ω- Bring your attention to your belly. If it's tight, recognize your storyteller is holding on. Do the Candle Breath to access some long, deep out-breaths. Then allow a smile to go all the way down into your belly.

Partnering with Your Wisdom Self:

Asking for clarity from Life comes from knowing that you are not alone. You have a wisdom self within you that has been with you every step of the way. The more you access your wisdom self, the more you discover you are not the one in charge of your healing. To think that you are is like a peach tree trying to create its peaches (and feeling it is not doing it well enough or fast enough)! Life is in charge of Life and just as the forces of Life are working together to bring forth a peach; they are also working together in your life to bring you into consciousness.

You can access the wisdom self within you through asking questions without looking for an answer. This can be frustrating in the beginning because you are so used to trying to find an answer. But answers of this kind come from your mind which has a limited capacity to understand what is truly going on. To ask questions of Life bypasses your struggling mind and is one of the most powerful tools you will be given by Life.

You can ask these kinds of questions as you move throughout your day. The one I use the most is "What do I need to say, do or be in this situation that is for the highest good?" It still delights me to see the depth of wisdom that moves through me when I turn it over to Life. I say and do things I couldn't even comprehend the moment before I asked Life for clarity.

Questions can be helpful in taking you right to what you are experiencing. Here is an example from a woman in one of my phone groups:

> It's been a pretty stressful, anxious time lately. Yesterday I stopped by the grocery store after work to pick up a couple things for dinner. I saw a little display touting this black Finnish licorice, and all of a sudden I HAD to have licorice. After some debate, I put it in my basket, and while I was waiting in the checkout line, I was thinking about how I could eat it in the car, and how good it would taste, and how nobody would know that I'd had it.

Finally I noticed that my stomach was getting tighter and tighter, but I still wanted licorice. By the time I got to the car, I was noticing my stomach more and the licorice a bit less. As I sat down behind the wheel, I put both my hands on my belly and asked, "What am I experiencing right now?" My attention immediately settled into the tightness in my stomach and I said to it, "I see you. I don't know what you're trying to tell me, but I see you, and I'll try to listen." Suddenly I didn't need to eat the licorice, and it wasn't even particularly interesting anymore. I drove home, made dinner and ate it with my family – all without licorice.

Her willingness to ask Life for clarity in seeing what was going on inside of her lessened the grip of the spells she was experiencing and instead opened her up to curiosity. As it became interesting to bring her attention to the tightness in her stomach, her heart woke up and began to give the tightness the compassionate acceptance it was longing for. Through being seen, the urge to numb herself through licorice became less interesting than being with herself. And all of this happened from the willingness to ask a question!

It is amazing how most people, when faced with a challenge, totally forget that their wisdom self is there within them, waiting to be of assistance! The types of questions to ask are: "What is asking to be met here?" or "What am I ready to see?" or "What is the way through this?" You can ask these when what is arising within you is too big to unhook from and you are caught in resistance, when it is unclear exactly what is going on, or when Life is moving too fast for you to take the time to turn your attention within and see what is going on.

The power of these questions is in the questions themselves. They signal Life that you are ready to listen to wisdom that comes from beyond your mind and that you are ready to see what you formerly resisted. Remember, whenever you ask this kind of question, you set things in motion. In the beginning of tapping into the power of asking questions without looking for an answer, your mind will look for answers, doubt that they will come, and maybe even give up easily saying, "This doesn't work." But it does work and answers will come to you in Life's time and in Life's way. And they will come.

> -Ω- Ask Life what it is that you are ready to see inside of you and then let that question go to work its magic from underneath your everyday awareness.

The Healing of Your Heart:

With the spells that don't let go under the light of your attention, you will begin to see that they are asking for the healing of your heart, for you can finally see how scared, angry, lost and lonely your storyteller is. The more you learn how to be curious and ask Life for clarity, the more your heart will naturally open. When the formerly unacceptable parts of yourself are met with your aware heart, (all is welcome here) this is where lasting healing occurs.

It is your heart that knows how to embrace rather than resist your experience. Remember, we accessed the powerful healing of the heart in the last chapter through: "All is welcome here," "As is. I'm here," and "I see you. I'm here." The heart is the place where you move beyond fighting with what is and instead give it the space that it needs to move through you. It is the heart that naturally knows the acceptance, spaciousness, and listening that every single part of you is longing for.

There is a healing story from a woman in one of my groups about the power of noticing that you are caught in reaction, the willingness to ask questions, and the ability of your aware heart to heal the deepest of holdings inside of you.

> -Ω- As you hear this story, the invitation is to put your hand over your heart to remind yourself to meet whatever arises within you with accepting attention.

I live with my Grandmother who is 86 and she usually awakens by 9:30 in the morning. I've never seen her get up later than 10:30 in the six months I've been her caretaker. In the quiet of the morning, as time slowly approached the 10:30 mark, my storyteller began to weave its tale. "She never sleeps this late. It is strange that she isn't up yet, don't you think?" Rather than hooking into its story, I took a deep breath, placed my hand over my heart, and said "Hello" to this fear-based story, reminding it that it is welcome here.

This time the storyteller didn't want to be interrupted, so it continued to tell an even more entrancing story. "It's unusually quiet. I can't hear her snoring, and I usually hear her get up and use the bathroom in the night and I didn't. She has died in her sleep. She's dead! My grandmother is dead. I know it. I can feel it! I don't want to lose her and now I won't have a place to live, so what am I going to do?" I could feel myself getting drawn back into my stories of fear.

Heart pounding, neck and shoulders tensed, arms closed across a tight belly, my curiosity woke up again and brought me out of reaction. "This is just the storyteller," it says. My shoulders drop slightly and I invite my neck to relax. One hand on my heart, and another on my softening belly, I say, "Who's here?" Immediately it is clear that it is the scared one. "Oh, Sweetheart," I say, "it's okay that you're here. We're safe. Life is in charge, and all is well."

As my belly softens, my shoulders relax and I open into the spaciousness of touching my fear with my heart. Then the stories arise again. For 45 minutes this dance continued, the lyrics from the storyteller increasing in detail, and the rhythm from my breath and my willingness to be compassionately curious about what the storyteller was doing being a steady anchor.

Tightness would overtake, and then I would soften around it. It was like watching a wave hit its peak and then recede. I was not the wave with its troughs and peaks. I was the witness of the wave in all its beauty and glory, and it was breathtaking and magnificent to watch.

As it approached 11:00, which was when I decided to check on her, the storyteller was building more elaborate plots. It would close around fear, and then my heart would accept it, allowing it and not needing to change it. Then I would watch it build again and then there was the heart to envelop it in love. With every wave, the heart deepened until the storyteller was completely enveloped in love.

As I opened her door, I heard her deep breathing and then the loud ring from the phone on her nightstand. As she jumped up and answered the phone I shut the door, smiling at the truly rich gift she had given me by sleeping in. Then my storyteller said, "Oh, I'm so stupid, I thought she was dead. I made such a big deal out of nothing." And my heart responded, "Oh, Sweetheart. I love you just as you are!" The dance continues.

When she shared her experience with me, I asked her to write it down so I could include it in the book. She wrote at the end of it, "A whole cast of characters have shown up in this experience, and amazingly, I have greeted each one into my heart with love and open arms. And you know, *not one stayed very long*! Even with the one inside of me that believed that I wouldn't be able to write down this experience in the right way (and thus I am doing life wrong), I could lovingly remind her that Life is doing life and it is safe."

She concluded, "To let it all go, and to trust this process; not to be caught in any of the stories that were trying to catch me yesterday; to have the openness and love in my heart to allow them to pass through me; and to continue to return over and over to my truth that Life is for us and it is trustable - what a game-changer and peace bringer. I am so filled with gratitude!"

Even with her storyteller caught in a deep spell of fear, she was able to realize that it was just her storyteller and give it the compassionate attention it needed. When you recognize the powerful healing that comes when you can meet your experience with your heart, there will still be times where your heart won't open. Know that noticing you are caught in your storyteller and turning it over to Life are enough. These are the foundational tools of awakening. And the more you turn toward yourself, the more your heart will effortlessly open.

It is very important *not to force* the opening of your heart. Now that you know how powerful it is to touch your experience with your heart, your mind will try to do your heart. ("I am saying 'I see you' and nothing is happening," says the mind.) But it doesn't work to give your accepting attention in hopes that something will let go. The bound up parts inside of you are very sensitive even to subtle feelings of wanting them to go away. True letting go happens when something is fully seen and fully accepted, and, if needed, fully heard *without it needing to be any different than it is.*

One of the biggest moments in the healing of my fear came when, with deep sincerity, I said to the scared one inside of me, "If you need to be here my whole Life that is okay!" Looking back at that time, I can see now that my fear calmed down dramatically after it was met in that way.

So we're not trying to make something happen. This is about using your mind in a new way: using it to meet with your heart what is going on rather than trying to fix it. This is about moments of purely relating to your experience. Those moments culminate in a shift of perception that brings healing beyond anything you can even imagine right now. Under the gaze of accepting attention the energy that was bound up inside of you is transformed back into the free-flowing aliveness it came from.

> -Ω- Turn your attention to yourself and be curious about what you are experiencing right now. Allow your experience to develop like a Polaroid picture. Whatever you notice – a feeling, a sensation or story – say to it, "I see you."

The Doorway of Discomfort:

In order to know and live from the spaciousness of the meadow, it is important to change your relationship with discomfort. Rather than resisting it, you go toward it. You move beyond wanting to hold it at bay or falling into it. By moving toward it, whatever is happening becomes workable rather than taking you over. When you realize the healing that comes from standing with what you have formerly run way from, you become a 'tightness' detective. Whenever your mind, body or heart is tight, it is guaranteed that you are resisting your experience, caught in being identified with your storyteller with all of its spells. Remember, anything that makes you tight is of the fight (of the cloud bank of struggle).

The more you awaken out of your storyteller, you realize there is nothing worth closing around. Rather than tightening around your discomfort, you finally see that you do not want all of your conditioned stories to be fueled through your identification with them. Nor do you want them stuffed back inside of you where they can create all sorts of havoc. So you finally discover that the only choice is to experience what you are experiencing *as it is*, giving it your accepting attention so the bound up energy has the space to move through you. Immeasurable joy results from recognizing a familiar story of struggle for what it is, just a conditioned story, instead of following it down the rabbit hole! And in that recognition lies the possibility of the bound up energy of the spell opening up so it can be freed up to move through you rather than being stuffed down inside of you again.

Yes, there are many deeply hidden parts that are painful when they come close to the surface, and it is the most uncomfortable states that need you the most. Once, when I was talking about the power of saying, "I see you," a woman in one of my groups reported that she heard it as "I.C.U." (Intensive Care Unit). She then started laughing at the irony of that, for she recognized that the parts of her that most need to hear "I see you" are the ones that have been in survival mode the longest (and thus are in the I.C.U.). They desperately need to be heard. They need you to respond to your experience with as much curiosity and compassion as you can muster.

When you are meeting your deepest holdings, turning toward your experience can be likened to what happens when your hand gets so cold on a winter's day that your fingers turn white from the blood vessels contracting. When you put your fingers in warm water and the blood begins to flow back in, it hurts like hell! At times that is what it is like when the energy begins to flow again in your body and heart. As your attention touches and opens up the bound up parts of yourself, it can hurt. But this is the hurt of healing. Just as your hand feels alive again after the blood flows back in, you feel much more alive when the bound up parts of you begin to open up again.

If it is a very painful part that is asking for your attention, it helps to breathe into the experience, opening it up from the inside with the gentle caress of your breath. It also helps to remember that nothing lasts. Every thought, feeling and sensation you have ever had has eventually moved through you. It will all pass through much more quickly when it is met with your heart. Remember, this is just bound up energy that wants to move rather than being caught in the web of your resistance. Know that your heart is up to the task of opening to it.

A woman with whom I have worked for a while shared an experience with me that speaks directly to the joy of meeting even the deepest of spells inside of us:

-Ω- As you read this story, check in with your breath and notice if it is holding. If so, allow one long "Ahh" breath.

I went into a contracted place after a friend's death. The contrast to the openness and expansion I had been feeling was painful and I was struggling with it. I turned my attention inside and asked who was here and a terrified one showed up! It was a new feeling – an intense feeling of terror – and it was connected to dying. I realized my mind was terrified of dying, and my friend's death has allowed me to see this part. I didn't even know it was here to that degree. I couldn't see or feel it before because I had pushed it away so thoroughly. But it's been on a low simmer underneath my everyday awareness for a very long time.

Even though I had been working with the scared one, welcoming it in and feeling pretty good about it, on this occasion my mind was screaming. This part felt like being trapped in a small room trying to escape/get out by frantically banging against the walls. It felt hard to breathe, but rather than running away, I just noticed it. I felt all of the feelings without trying to change anything.

I talked to it; "Of course sweetie, of course you would be here. You see death as the end, so why wouldn't you be terrified. Let's get to know each other. I'm sorry I haven't really seen you before this. You are beautiful. All is welcome here. You are welcome here. You are well...come here."

I felt such tenderness for it in that moment. I held it in my heart and let it be. I even told it that it could stay here as long as it needed to – and I meant it. It was an incredible experience.

I am excited to get to know my terrified one better and to develop a relationship with it. I've sat with it every morning, connecting, saying hello. Such a gift! Such a gift!

-Ω- Notice what her willingness to explore terror brought up inside of you. Then give whatever you are experiencing the gift of a smile!

She could say "What a gift!" because the hidden terror that had influenced her from underneath her everyday awareness her whole life was finally seen and enfolded in her heart. Also, the energy that was bound up in the terror and in her resistance to it was freed up, bringing her back to the joy and the spaciousness of the meadow of her being. She trusted Life enough to open up to this terror so it could let go, which brings us back to the core message of this book: **Life is set-up, to bring up, what has been bound up, so it can open up, to be freed up, so you can show up for Life!**

A Gradual Awakening:

Know that each moment of curiosity and each moment of compassion matters! I call this the "bucket syndrome." Every time you meet your experience, it is like a drop of water in a bucket that is sitting at your feet. After a few times of turning toward your experience, you look down and there are a couple of drops of water in the bucket. So your mind says, "This is not working." But as you continue to be drawn to being compassionately curious, one day you look down and the bucket is half full, every drop of water representing a moment of curiosity. Still, the mind will say this is not enough. But one day, you feel unexplainable joy and you discover your foot is wet! The bucket is overflowing.

In this journey of discovering how to bring your accepting attention to whatever you are experiencing, one day you may notice you're caught, and not remember to turn it over. Another day you may come across something that is so deep and disturbing to your mind that you can barely recognize that you are caught and not know what to do except turn it over to Life. Other days you can easily notice the lump in your throat and it lets go just through being seen. Then there will be times when you can recognize the tightness in your neck, and not have a clue about what it is expressing.

The deeper you move into awakening, there will be times that core spells are easily seen and easily heard, releasing the energy that was formerly bound up in them. Your whole body will then glow with the energy that has been opened. It is important to know that whatever opens up for you, you can be with yourself for just seconds or you can spend half an hour exploring your immediate experience. Trust what is calling to you.

Also, there will be times you don't want to turn toward your experience. When you are caught in the reactions of your spells, you want to get rid of them, get lost in them or blame others for causing them. The question I ask you is, "Has this ever brought you the peace you long for?" In the short run, it may bring you the feeling of getting away from what you don't want to look at and it may also give you the illusion of control. In the long run, however, it just keeps you caught in your storyteller, cutting you off from the meadow of your being.

As you become willing to be curious and give your immediate experience the accepting attention that is woven all throughout this book, you discover an amazing thing: healing doesn't come from fixing, changing or getting rid of anything. It doesn't even come from letting go of anything. It comes when these formerly bound up parts receive full acceptance and *they let go*! This is why Rumi in the last half of his much-quoted poem *The Guest House* said, "Learn the alchemy that few human beings know. As soon as you accept what difficulties you have been given, a door opens." He is not talking about a mental acceptance. He is inviting you to accept that the difficulty is an essential part of your journey and in this acceptance, you can then explore it. And in that exploration, what was bound up in the difficulty, opens up (a door opens)!

So in this process of discovering the doorways that are always embedded in the parts of yourself that you have tried the most to stay away from, please remember that awakening isn't so much something you do as something you discover that you are. Your natural state is curiosity, and all we are doing here is waking it up so it can dispel (remove the spells from) the cloud banks of your conditioning.

RE-MEMBERING SECTION

Re-membering Session

You may have discovered in last week's sessions that there were certain experiences, stories in your head, sensations in your body, or deep feelings, that didn't quiet down when you were with them through moments of saying, "I see you." The parts of your cloud bank that keep on grabbing your attention are just trapped energy, and they are asking for listening so they can let go.

This is the time to create a relationship with whatever you are experiencing through saying, "Tell me about your world." Remember, all of these parts of you are just like you. Whether it is a busy mind that wants to plan the rest of the day, or an ache in your stomach, or a lump of tears in your throat, or a feeling of anxiousness in your chest, each of these parts have a particular view of the world, a view that was most likely formed and frozen inside of you when you were young. And just like you, they calm down when they are heard. When you can bring your aware heart to your experience, giving it the kind of listening it needs to let go, your cloud bank thins and the meadow is more available to you.

It is important to remember that you are not trying to make anything happen here. The parts of you that are longing to be heard are very sensitive to the slightest desire that, if you listen to them, they will go away. You are not trying to let go of anything or make anything let go. That comes from the old paradigm that believes that if you fix, change or get rid of whatever is arising inside of you, then you will know peace. This doesn't work. In fact, it actually energizes what you are trying to get beyond. You are simply interested in listening, in a compassionate way, to what draws you away from your breath. And in that listening, the energy bound up in that feeling/thought/sensation is given the space to begin to move and let go when it is ready.

After you read the following section, put the book down, close your eyes and begin exploring. If timing your session, add one minute, taking it to 12 minutes. If time is not an issue, stay with each step as long as your curiosity is engaged.

Let's begin:

- Close your eyes and dip the finger of your attention into the river of your experience, noticing what it is like to be you right now.

- For three in-breaths, tighten your muscles and then *very slowly* relax everything on your out-breath as you say the great sound of letting go, "Ahh!"

- Bring your attention to the circle of your breath, saying the calming/focusing words, "In...Out; Deep...Slow; Calm...Ease; As is...I'm here." Or, "As is...I'm here" by itself.

When you notice your attention has drifted away from the circle of your breath and the calming/focusing words, ask yourself, "What is asking to be seen?" This question is about turning your attention toward yourself in this very moment and looking clearly into your own experience.

If you notice a feeling/sensation/story, explore it with the finger of your attention. Say to whatever you are noticing, "I see you. It is okay that you are here. I want to know about your world." Remember, every single part of us has a view of the world, a view that was formed before we were six. And these parts respond to being heard just like you do. So these words are inviting you to be fully with whatever is there without falling into it, giving it the healing of your own heart.

Whatever story/feeling/sensation you are exploring may be ready to share with you its view of the world. Don't force this. Let it come naturally. If nothing happens, know that it has heard your willingness to hear about its world and will share it with you when it is ready.

Stay with this curiosity for as long as it interests you, from a few seconds to a few minutes. If you find yourself getting fuzzy, let the exploration go and come back to the circle of your breath.

If you can't see clearly what is taking you away, know that asking, "What is asking to be seen?" will set things in motion and simply bring your attention back to the circle of your breath.

- At the end, expand your awareness and be curious about your experience after having given yourself the healing of your own attention.

- When you are ready, open your eyes.

Abbreviated Version:

- Close your eyes and check in, noticing what it is like to be you right now.

- For three in-breaths, tighten your muscles and then *very slowly* relax everything on your out-breath as you say the great sound of letting go, "Ahh!"

- Bring your attention to the circle of your breath, saying the calming/focusing words, In...Out; Deep...Slow; Calm...Ease; As is...I'm here." Or "As is...I'm here" by itself.

- When you notice your attention has drifted away from the circle of your breath and the calming/focusing words, ask yourself, "What is asking to be seen?"

- If you notice something, explore it with the finger of your attention and say to it, "I see you. It is okay that you are here. I want to know about your world."

- Stay with this curiosity for as long as it interests you. If you find yourself getting fuzzy, let the exploration go and come back to the circle of your breath.

- At the end, expand your awareness and be curious about your experience after having given yourself the healing of your own attention.

- When you are ready, open your eyes.

Re-memberings

- By learning how to turn toward your experience rather than away from it, you access the powerful healing force of your own heart.

- The energy that was tightly held in all the spells you took on can now be released, and the more you release, the more you naturally rediscover the meadow of your being.

- The most powerful way to open up the bound up energy is with your attention, for when your attention and your immediate experience come together, bound up energy begins to move.

- All that we have explored is about being curious around what you are experiencing rather than trying to fix, get rid of or understand.

- You are not alone. You have a wisdom self within you that has been with you every step of the way. The more you access it, you also discover you are not the one in charge of your healing.

- The heart is the place where you move beyond fighting with what is and instead give it the space that it needs to move through.

- Become a 'tightness detective' because what makes you tight is of the fight (of the cloud bank). Go toward discomfort. Then everything becomes workable rather than taking you over.

- The more you awaken out of the cloud bank, the more you realize there is nothing worth closing around.

- You don't want your conditioned stories to be fueled through identifying with them nor do you want them stuffed back inside of you where they can create all sorts of havoc.

- As your attention begins to touch and open up the bound up parts of yourself, it can hurt. But this is the hurt of healing.

- This isn't about trying to make something happen. This is about moments of pure relating with your experience and this brings healing beyond anything you can even imagine right now.

- Healing doesn't come from fixing, changing, getting rid of or even letting go of anything. It comes when these formerly bound up parts receive full acceptance and *they let go*!

CHAPTER 9

Life is For You

Throughout this book we have been exploring a radical shift of perception: the healing you long for doesn't come from changing anything. It comes from the ability to see and be with what is, for who you are is awareness. You are the space that your storyteller is happening in. As awareness, you can see the spells, feelings and sensations that pass through you all day long rather than being lost in the stories they generate.

When you learn how to be curious about what is going on inside of you, you discover the ability to experience what you are experiencing without turning it into a problem. You can then give the energy that was bound up in your struggles the attention and the spaciousness it needs in order to let go. This brings you back to the free-flowing aliveness that you truly are – the meadow of your being.

In order to be this curious about what is going on rather than always trying to control it, it is important to know that your life is *for you*. Life is not just a random series of events that happen because you did it right or you did it wrong. Instead, it is an intelligent unfolding that is revealing itself to you all day long, bringing you step-by-step from unconsciousness to consciousness.

Take a moment now to feel how different that is from the way you usually perceive Life: as something happening to you that needs to be controlled, fixed and changed. Imagine what it would be like to let go of the whole game of resisting Life and instead to trust it. In this trust you could then open to it, listen to it, and grow from every encounter.

At the last Hawaii retreat I led on the island of Molokai, the core focus of the retreat was "All Is Welcome Here." On the second day, one of the participants said that whenever that phrase was spoken, she heard "All is well. Come here!" When you learn how to stop trying to make your life be what you want it to be and show up for it instead (*All Is Welcome Here*), you discover that all is well (the meadow is always with you and Life knows what it is doing) and it is safe to be here. You can show up for the life that Life is giving you!

When Eben Alexander woke up from his seven-day coma, the first thing he said to his sister was, "All is well!" In order to open to "All Is Well" so you can truly be here for Life, it is important to recognize that the evolution which is unfolding on the Earth includes human beings. Everything is a part of this evolution, including you. You are Life evolving from unconsciousness to consciousness. Your life is not a random series of events. It is an intelligent and mysterious process that is *for* Life.

I like to call it the "flawless, methodical mystery." It is flawless because each and every experience of your life is tailor-made to wake you up out of your unconsciousness. Also, it is truly methodical. There are basic steps we all go through on our journey out of the cloud bank of our minds back into recognition of the meadow of Life. And it is truly mysterious. Without fully understanding it, we can open to it, rediscovering what Joseph Campbell describes as "the rapture of being alive."

The Six Phases of Consciousness:

Your life is a journey from unconsciousness to consciousness. Michael Beckwith, minister of the Agape Church, describes this evolution in four phases. I have added two more, "Life happens in you" and "Life happens for you," and call them the "Six Phases of Consciousness."

- Life happens to you.
- Life happens by you.
- Life happens in you.
- Life happens for you.
- Life happens through you.
- Life is you.

Let us take a few minutes to explore each one. I invite you, as you read, to keep on checking in with yourself. You are being given important information in this chapter. Remember that the most powerful thing you can do for your healing is to have your attention and your experience together, even as you are reading this book and no matter what it brings up for you.

-Ω- Dip the finger of your attention into the river of your experience. Allow whatever is here to be here. You have never experienced Life quite like this and never will again. This moment in your life is unique, and it is okay exactly as it is.

Life Happens To You:

For a good deal of your life you have probably lived like most human beings, feeling that Life is happening *to you*. Life is so big and if you are honest with yourself, you never really know what is going to happen next. You wake up one morning and your heart is light and happy and the next day you're unsettled. Bosses fire you, the flu debilitates you, people you love reject you, every day you get a little older and death is always lurking around the corner.

So it is understandable that the more unconscious you are, the more often you feel like a victim to Life. When you live in the belief that Life is happening to you, you often view it as a possible threat. So you stay caught in your head, finding yourself lost in your storyteller that resists, reacts, defends and explains, hoping to figure everything out. It generally does absolutely anything except be open to Life, right here, right now.

Life Happens By You:

When it becomes too uncomfortable to live with this much powerlessness, you evolve into the belief that Life is happening *by you*. Rather than being a victim to Life, you believe you can control it. There can be a great feeling of personal power in this level of consciousness. It is a necessary step in moving out of the victimhood of the first stage, but people get caught there. Men try to control women and vice versa. Religions try to control the masses. Countries try to control other countries. The majority of people try to control others who are not like them (gay, different skin color, dissimilar religions). Most of all, we try to control ourselves, hoping to make ourselves be what we think we should be.

There is an enormous amount of effort in this level of consciousness. The storyteller believes that in order for anything good to happen it has to *make it happen*. So it loves to set goals and feels very ashamed when it doesn't follow through (just think of New Year's resolutions!) The storyteller eventually evolves into intentions. Goals are where you use your mind to try to make things be the way you want them. With intentions, you work with feeling what you want to generate. None of this is bad or wrong. These are important tools to use on the path of awakening and sometimes they actually work. But what would happen if you recognized that, rather than trying to make things happen, opening into Life will bring you what you most deeply long for!

There is a relatively new form of control where you believe you can control your reality. In this form of control, the storyteller says that all I have to do is think the right thoughts and I can make my life be the way I want it to be. The main difficulty with this is that, in the long run, it doesn't work. To think you can control Life is like being a cork in the ocean believing it can control the movement of the ocean. Yes, it does change the movement of the water right where it is, but it can't influence all the other powerful forces that make up the ocean.

To stay caught in this phase of consciousness is to be cut off from the creative flow of Life. Believing that you are in charge of Life, you are mainly identified with your conceptual world, trying to create a reality rather than showing up for reality.

When you have lived this level of consciousness long enough, you see the downside of it. First, you find yourself becoming fearful of your thoughts: I shouldn't be thinking this way because I will manifest this in my world. Second, it can also bring forth shame, for when it doesn't work the way the books promise, you think this is because you haven't done it right enough or well enough. Author and speaker Carolyn Myss, who used to teach that you could manifest what you want if you just think right, evolved beyond that. When she was in Seattle in the 1990's she asked an audience of 600 to raise their hands if they had been able to create the reality they wanted. Not one person did!

-Ω- As you are reading about *to you* and *by you*, your belly may have tightened again. Allow any holding you discover there to melt away. Smile and let this softening move all the way down into your pelvic floor and around to your back.

Life Happens In You:

You eventually begin to see that all of your reacting and controlling hasn't brought you the ease and joy you long for. Instead of being the victim to your life and or needing to make it be any particular way, which is the endless game of struggle, you begin to get an inkling that Life is something to be listened to, opened to. This is where you start evolving into the next step, where Life is happening in you.

At this level of consciousness you begin to realize something very startling: most of the time, rather than experiencing Life, you think about it, seeing only the thoughts in your head! When you experience Life through your thoughts, you stop experiencing it as it is. Or, as the well-known French author Anais Nin once said, "We don't see things as they are. We see them as we are." You project your spells onto yourself and others rather than really seeing what is. When was the last time you truly saw a loved one's face? If you are honest with yourself, it has probably been a long time.

It is in this phase that you also realize that your suffering doesn't come from the experiences of your life. Instead it comes from your *stories about what is happening*. It comes from inside of you! There could be a gray day and you're just fine. Then on another gray day you could be miserable. You may say it is because the day is gray, but it comes from your story about the day, not the day itself.

This is where you begin to live what we have been calling the *you-turn*. You become less interested in being a victim to your life or even trying to make it be any different than it is. You realize that the healing you long for comes when you turn your attention within. When you get to know the spells that are the source of your suffering, you can unhook from them and come back to Life.

-Ω- Do a *you-turn* and ask, "What is asking to be seen?" Be curious about what sits here right now.

Life Happens For You:

The more you become curious about what is happening rather than reacting and controlling, the more you come to a wonderful realization that your life is *for* you. Rather than Life being something that is happening to you that you must control, you realize there are no ordinary moments!

Life is not a random series of events. It is a highly intelligent unfolding that is putting you in the exact situations you need in order to see and unhook from the spells that keep you separate from its flow. No matter what is happening in your life, you finally understand that Life knows what it is doing.

Rather than Life being something you have to mold and shape into what you want it to be, you begin to show up for Life exactly as it is. Yes, the flow of Life includes pain, loss and death. But resisting the pains of Life only turn them it into suffering, and the suffering that comes from resistance is always much greater than directly experiencing your pain. Instead of tightening around your experiences and turning away from them, which only thickens your cloud bank of struggle, you bring your attention to your experience, whatever it is.

Even little moments of curiosity about what is going on right now sprinkled throughout your day are powerful! Every time you respond rather than react to what is going on inside of you, what was formerly bound up begins to loosen. Remember, your natural state is free-flowing aliveness. When that aliveness gets trapped in the spells, your energy and joy dim. When the spells receive the light of your attentiveness, they let go, and the trapped energy flows freely, bringing with it the bliss of openness. Remember: Life is setup, to bring up, what has been bound up, so it can open up, to be freed up, so you can show up for Life!

-Ω- Close your eyes for a few moments and open into this living moment of your life. Hear it, sense it, feel it. This is the only moment that matters in your whole life for it is the only moment where Life is happening!

Life Happens Through You:

The *for you* phase shows you that there is no such thing as an ordinary moment in your life and helps you to see that Life is speaking to you at all moments. Becoming curious about what you are experiencing and giving it the light of compassionate attention so it can let go, you evolve into the next phase of allowing Life to move *through you*. This is where you recognize that Life is trustable. It is not always likable, but it knows what it is doing.

Imagine a life where you trust Life implicitly. Every morning you wake up with a sense of adventure. Your belly is soft, your mind is curious and your heart is open. Rather than struggling with Life, you open to it, even when you are facing deep challenges. If you find yourself caught in reaction, you give your reaction the attention it needs to let go.

Just as when you unkink a hose, the vibrant flow of energy that is Life can now move freely *through you* and this brings forth the joy and aliveness you so deeply long for. Creativity that you could never imagine on your own becomes clear to you, blessing yourself and everyone you meet with the wisdom of the meadow of Life.

You experience deep gratitude for absolutely everything. You see that your life is dependent on every ounce of creativity that has ever happened in the universe. You also see that all that has happened to you, even the difficult, has been a part of your journey back into Life. Step-by-step Life is bringing you into consciousness, into the ability to be fully here for Life. Now you can relax and show up for the adventure. As Cynthia Bourgeault so beautifully says in her book *Mystical Hope*, "You find your way by being sensitively and sensually connected to exactly where you are, letting 'here' reach out and lead you."

Life Is You:

The more you can stand with Life, allowing it to move through you rather than reacting to it or controlling it, the more you begin to get glimpses of the sixth phase in which you see that Life is you. You are no longer a separate being. Instead, you merge completely back into the creative flow of Life, understanding that everything – every rock, person, cloud, molecule and ladybug – is you. You are Life! As Eckhart Tolle said, "You are not in the Universe; you are the universe, an intrinsic part of it. Ultimately you are not a person, but a focal point where the universe is becoming conscious of itself. What an amazing miracle."

-Ω- All is well. Come here.

As you look closely at the Six Phases of Consciousness, you will see that the first two are about fixing, changing, resisting and trying to control Life (Life is happening to you and by you). These phases are the world of your storyteller that doesn't want what is here (doesn't know how to open to Life) and wants what is not here (I can have what I want if I just think right). Throughout both of these phases, there is a veil between you and the living experience of Life because neither phase is about showing up for the creative river of Life.

The next two phases of consciousness are about using your mind to be curious about what is happening rather than resisting and controlling. In *Life is happening in you*, you recognize that the storyteller inside of you is what separates you from Life. So rather than trying to change anything, you become interested in what you are experiencing in any given moment. The more you are here for Life, the easy and the difficult, the joyous and the sorrowful, unhooking from all of your spells, the more clear it becomes that Life knows what it is doing and it is *for* you.

The final two phases of consciousness are all about coming home to the meadow. The more you live the truth that Life is *for* you, the more you relax into the flow, bringing you to the joy of Life moving *through* you. As your cloud bank dissipates, you not only recognize the meadow again, you recognize that *you are the meadow*! Life is you and you are Life!

Most people live in the first two phases, *to you* and *by you*, never knowing that right in the middle of these beliefs is a doorway into the last four. Life is waking you up from the contraction of the first two and into the opening of the last four. This is not only for your own healing, but for the healing of all beings, because as you see through your cloud bank of struggle, you become a healing presence in the world.

There is a paradoxical truth that is important to acknowledge. Human beings are evolving from the first phase to the sixth. It is also true that most days you will experience a number of these phases. It is not about getting rid of any particular phase or making one better than the other. They are all part of Life, and as you evolve, you will recognize and be able to embrace them all.

The Truth of Trust:

In order to evolve into and through the last four phases, the tattered threads of your trust of Life need to be rewoven. You, like most people, don't trust Life! It certainly feels untrustworthy. Life breaks your heart, brings illnesses to your body, and feels, at times, as though it gives you way more than you can handle.

If you don't trust it, how can you show up for it, opening to all that it is offering you in every experience you have? How can you allow it to bring you, step-by-step, from unconsciousness to consciousness? There is a shift of perception that will help you immensely in relearning how to trust Life, discovering that your life, rather than being something that needs to be controlled, is something that can be opened to. The shift is: Life is smarter than you!

Most of us are so caught in our storyteller that we live in a small world. What we pay attention to all day long is the cloud bank around our heads that is made out of our spells. We don't see what is going on here! And we definitely don't recognize the meadow.

As a means of opening your awareness from the tight and small world of your storyteller into a more spacious perspective, I invite you into what I call a big-picture exploration. Imagine you are sitting on the moon, looking at the beautiful blue-green jewel that is our planet. See it as a living being that has been unfolding for 4 ½ billion years. Look beyond it into the black, velvety depth of space that is filled with more stars than there are grains of sand on every beach of the Earth!

Now bring your attention back to the Earth floating in front of you, and as you drink in its beauty, recognize that absolutely everything on this planet was created from atoms that come from the stars – and that includes you! So everything you see is made out of stardust!

Now in your imagination, see the evolution of Earth as a movie. At its inception it was just a ball of gas and dust. Fast-forward the movie in your mind's eye and see land and water appearing as the Earth's atmosphere forms. Then see Life beginning to come together into various rudimentary beings in the seas. Now see Life crawl out of the seas and onto the continents as a wave of green flows across the formerly barren land. Insects appear, animals emerge and dinosaurs come and go.

In the evolution of Life on this planet, there was a time when there were no creatures with thumbs, so Life could not be picked up to be used and explored. Now see life evolving a few million years ago into a form that had two arms with fingers and thumbs, along with the kind of brain that was interested in picking up Life and exploring It. Life had never shown up in this way before!

Now see early human beings coming together into tribes. As their frontal lobes became more complex, see them discovering language, figuring out how to use tools, cultivating the land, creating villages and towns, and then creating the wheel and ships that sail across the oceans.

Fast-forward the movie again to just a few hundred years ago. See one set of your great, great, great grandparents being born, growing up, discovering one another, birthing one half of the partnership of your great, great grandparents and then disappearing back into mystery. This same cycle brought forth your grandparents, your parents and then you. Now see yourself appearing out of mystery at the exact place on this planet where you were born. Watch yourself evolve from a baby, to a young child, to a teenager and then into an adult.

As you are watching the movie of your life, bring it to this morning when you woke up, began your day and eventually came to the moment where you are reading this book. Realize that all of the millions of moments of your life have unfolded to this moment and this moment is the leading edge of the wave of evolution on this planet. Open to the knowing that this moment is no ordinary moment. Right here, right now, you are being given a very rare gift: the phenomenal gift of Life. For a short slice of time you get to be here, and then you too will dissolve back into mystery and Life will continue to unfold.

-Ω- Pause for a moment and contemplate all of the creativity that has gone before you that allows you and everything around you to exist.

Your Story:

This movie about the unfolding of Life on this planet that we just explored is *your story*. You are a being who is an expression of 4 ½ billion years of Life evolving on this planet. You exist in this body because of the vast creativity that has gone before you. Let's take your eyes for example. The first ancestors of your eyes came from polyps on the oceans floors that created cells that were able to differentiate light and dark.

In between that first rudimentary step into seeing and your ability to see are vast amounts of creativity that allow you to see this book! And it is not just your eyes that are dependent on the entire ingenuity of Life. Your whole life, like everybody else's, is dependent on every single act of creativity that has ever happened on this planet.

It is amazing to recognize the creativity that enabled Life to take stardust and make this planet and everything on it, including you. It is even more astounding to see that as you sit here reading this book, you are a community of 70 trillion cells that pump blood through 65,000 miles of arteries and veins, send messages along your nerves at the speed of light, regulate hormones, repair cells and digest food without a single thought from you. If you doubt that there is an amazing Intelligence that permeates and penetrates all of Life, just acknowledge what is happening in your body right now.

Because you don't recognize the Intelligence at the heart of Life, you believe you are separate from it. Believing you are separate from it, you buy into the illusion that you must control it. As soon as you believe you must control it, you become cut off from it, losing sight of the joy of being open to Life.

You actually trust Life a lot. You trust it enough to beat your heart and breathe your breath. But you think that the Intelligence at the heart of Life has nothing to do with your daily life. You, like most people, bought into the arrogance of the human ego that says that it is in charge. Because of this belief in separation, you think your life is just a random series of events that you must mold and shape into what you think they should be.

What would happen if this was not so? What would your life look like if you understood that the same Intelligence that keeps the planets spinning, heals the cuts on your skin, and brings spring forth out of winter is with you every step of the way? Can you open to the possibility that this creative Intelligence is weaving your life out of the primal opposites of dark and light and it is giving you exactly what you need in order to evolve from unconsciousness to consciousness? What would it be like if you understood that the same awesome force of evolution that created this planet and brought Life out of the sea and onto land is working its magic in your life?

To get even an inkling of what we are exploring here will allow you to let go of that grip of control enough that you can begin to feel the magic of trusting your life. The more you trust it, the more you will show up for it, and the more you show up for it, the more you will see that Life is wiser than you and is bringing you the exact set of experiences you need in order to come back to Life.

> -Ω- Lift your eyes from the book and recognize that in the vastness of all time this moment will never be repeated, and you have the privilege to bear witness to it.

What It Looks Like To Trust Life:

When you realize that Life is smarter than you, Life becomes very interesting. Rather than being lost in your storyteller, you realize something very extraordinary is happening here: there are no ordinary moments in your life! You become much more alert to what is happening, both outside and inside of you. If one's life is like an iceberg, most people just pay attention to the part above the water while what is really going on is happening underneath the 'water level' of their everyday awareness.

It is true that you are driving, working, showering, cooking, arguing, making love, raising children, birthing and dying. But underneath it all is the unfolding of intelligent evolution, and you are a part of that. You are evolving from an unconscious human being into a conscious one. This is happening in every experience of your life - *every* experience! *Life is for Life.* It is supporting your shift from being asleep to being awake. Just as Life assists a peach tree in creating fruit by sustaining it with sun, rain, bees and the nourishment of the Earth, it is giving you exactly what you need in order to know the fruit of a conscious human being, which is the ability to be awake to Life.

Living from the truth that your life is for you, you begin to let go of the belief that your suffering is caused by something outside of you: other people, your job, the shape of your body, the kind of mate you have, the type of health you have, the kind of past you had, or the sort of mind you have. You begin to see that your suffering is coming from inside of you, caused by the spells. Yes, there are difficult things that happen in your life, but when you don't get lost in your stories about them, you respond to the situation, gathering the gifts that are always embedded in the challenges of your life.

As you awaken, you become less interested in trying to change anything in your life and more interested in what is going on inside of you, especially in difficult situations. You have a deeper sense of allowing Life to put you in the exact situations you need in order for the core spells that make up your storyteller to be brought to the surface of your awareness. It is there that you can see them, watch them in action, and discover that they are just spells that were conditioned into you when you were young and that you no longer need to buy into them.

It is almost as if these deep and ancient spells of fear, shame, doubt, jealousy, not being enough, loneliness, and anger, to name a few, are like champagne bubbles that have been trapped inside of you. As your resistance to experiencing them lessens, they begin to loosen, arising to the surface to be seen. As they are fully seen, they burst, and the energy that was formerly trapped in them lets go. Rather than being afraid of this purification process, you begin to welcome it as the longing to be fully awake to Life becomes stronger than the fear of your spells.

-Ω- Pause for a moment and check into your belly. Allow any holding you discover there to melt away and let a smile fill you with its healing presence. Allow this softening to move all the way down into your pelvic floor and around to your back.

The Joy of Response-ability:

Whether it is an illness, pain, a difficult neighbor, a compulsion, a financial crisis or any other challenging situation in your life, it can be initially threatening to your storyteller to take responsibility (the ability to respond) for your own experience. Old reactions that come from spells can be very strong. But you learn how to become like one of those three-foot tall inflatable dolls with a weight in the bottom. When you're in a difficult situation, you feel like the doll when it is hit and falls over. More and more quickly, however, you do the *you-turn*, becoming curious about what this is bringing up inside of you, and you bounce back up again just like the doll does.

This is where you truly begin to trust Life. You know that difficult situations are for you. You see that just as the body cleanses itself of foreign viruses and bacteria, your being will cleanse itself of the old spells. The more you want to see your spells, the more Life puts you in the situations that will bring them up so they can be touched enough with the light of your consciousness to let go. Thus you are no longer the victim to your life.

You will eventually have to meet the places within you that you are the most afraid of in order to heal. Remember the monster in the closet we explored in Chapter Five? You finally uncovered your eyes and looked at what you thought was a monster in your closet, only to discover it was a pile of clothing thrown in there. In the same way, feelings, sensations and stories become things to be curious about.

Even feelings like aloneness, or unending sadness, or the black hole of nothingness that seem so deep and real when you are resisting them become something to say "hello" to and touch with compassion. As you stand with them, they no longer have the power over you they used to have, and the energy that was bound up in them is released, opening you to the meadow that is always with you.

It is important to remember as you are bringing consciousness into your daily life that you have never left the meadow; you just thought that you had. All of the joy, clarity and aliveness you long for have always been with you, right here, right now. You just haven't seen it because your storyteller has grabbed hold of your attention and rarely let it go. The more you allow Life to put you in the situations that bring up the core spells of your storyteller, the more your cloud bank will thin and you will be able to recognize and live from the meadow of your being.

RE-MEMBERING SECTION

This week's Re-membering Statement:

Life is for me

Your Own Statement:

_____

Re-membering Session

For this week's session, come back to the meadow metaphor. In the meadow everything flows, for everything is energy. The same is true for you. The energy of Life flows through you as feelings, sensations and thoughts. The healing you long for comes when you allow Life to flow through you. You don't hold onto the comfortable and easy states and you don't tighten down around the uncomfortable and difficult.

All that you have been exploring in these sessions has led you to this place where you can open up the field of your attention, and rather than identifying with your stories/feelings/sensations, you become the space of awareness that allows all to simply pass through you.

We will begin with grounding your attention on your breath for just a few breaths, but then the invitation is to let go of your breath as a focus and allow curiosity to be your ground. This will feel a little bit like letting go of the steering wheel of a car. You are so used to trying to control life that you may even be trying to control your Re-membering Sessions! You may think a good one is when you stay on your focus and a bad one is when you don't. The invitation is to move beyond that and allow whatever is appearing to come and go without getting hooked by it. All is welcome here.

All sorts of things will arise inside of you and simply pass through you if you are curious. You will find that your attention will be drawn into your storyteller and the feelings and sensations that it generates, but then curiosity will naturally arise again. You may be lost in your storyteller for a number of minutes and then your natural curiosity will kick in again. If you don't judge yourself, then you will be able simply to be curious about what is happening.

Remember, you are not trying to create any particular experience. Rather than trying to make something happen, or thinking about what is happening, or resisting it, or trying to change it, you are using your mind simply to be curious about what is going on right now. Your inner world is like the weather, and as you learn how to be curious, the weather of your stories/feelings/sensations will pass through you like the clouds pass through the sky.

After you read the following section, put the book down, close your eyes and begin exploring. If timing your session, add one minute, taking it to 13 minutes. If time is not an issue, stay with each step as long as your curiosity is engaged.

Let's begin:

- Close your eyes and dip the finger of your attention into the river of your experience, noticing what it is like to be you right now.

- For at least three in-breaths, tighten your muscles and then *very slowly* relax everything on your out-breath as you say the great sound of letting go, "Ahh!"

- For a few breaths, bring your attention to the circle of your breath, saying the calming/focusing words, "In...Out; Deep... Slow; Calm...Ease; As is...I'm here" or "As is...I'm here" by itself.

- Let go of paying attention to your breath and allow curiosity to be your ground.

Anything could be going on: different sensations in your body, stories in your head, emotions passing through. For these few precious moments, let go of trying to make something happen or needing anything to be any different than what it is and just be interested. Let whatever is appearing arise and pass right through you.

In the beginning of your session, your mind may wander, thinking about the day, scared it's not doing the session right. But if you stay open, your natural curiosity will kick in and you will be interested in what is showing up inside of you. It can help to ask yourself throughout the session, "What am I paying attention to right now?" Be curious about what is before you think about it.

If you find yourself wandering a lot, ground in your breath for a few breaths and then open up the field of your attention again and be curious about what sits here right now. Stay with this curiosity as long as the mind is willing. It may be for 30 seconds or 30 minutes.

When you are ready, open your eyes.

Abbreviated Version:

- Close your eyes and check in, noticing what it is like to be you right now.

- For at least three in-breaths, tighten your muscles and then *very slowly* relax everything on your out-breath as you say the great sound of letting go, "Ahh!"

- For a few breaths, bring your attention to the circle of your breath, saying the calming/focusing words, "In...Out; Deep... Slow; Calm...Ease; As is...I'm here." Or, "As is...I'm here" by itself.

- Let go of riding the waves of your breath and open the field of your attention. Be curious about what is showing up inside of you, allowing whatever is here to be here.

- If you find yourself wandering a lot, ground in your breath for a few breaths and then open up the field of your attention again and be curious about what sits here right now.

- When you are ready, open your eyes.

Re-memberings

- Life is not a random series of events that happen because you did it right or wrong. It is an intelligent unfolding that is always speaking to you, waking you up.

- The first two phases of consciousness are about fixing, changing, resisting and trying to control Life (*Life is happening to you and by you*). They put a veil between you and Life.

- The next two are about curiosity. In *Life is happening in you*, you become interested in what you are experiencing. In *Life is for you*, you see that Life is putting you in the situations you need in order to see your spells.

- The final two phases are all about coming home to the meadow. The more you relax into the flow, the more it brings you to the joy of *Life moving through you*. As you reconnect with the meadow again, you recognize that everything is you.

- If you doubt the amazing Intelligence of Life, recognize that you are made of 70 trillion cells all working together, that your heart pumps blood through 65,000 miles of arteries and veins, and that your body heals cuts and digests food without a single thought from you!

- Because you don't recognize the Intelligence at the heart of Life, you believe you are separate from it. Believing you are separate from it, you buy into the illusion that you must control it.

- To even get an inkling of what we are exploring here will allow you to let go of the grip of control enough that you can begin to feel the magic of trusting your life.

- Your spells are like champagne bubbles trapped inside of you. As your resistance lessens, they loosen, rising to the surface to be seen so that the energy trapped in them can let go.

- Rather than being afraid of this purification process, you begin to welcome it, for the longing to come fully awake to Life becomes stronger than your fear of the spells.

- This is where you truly begin to trust Life. You know that difficult situations are for you. You see that just as the body cleanses itself of foreign viruses and bacteria, your being will cleanse itself of the old spells.

CHAPTER 10

The Song of the Heart

Will your cloud bank dissolve all of a sudden when you recognize what is being offered here? That has not been my experience or the experience of 99.999% of the people I have known over the years. It is, as Stephen Levine once described it, a gradual awakening. When asked by someone how long this would take, he responded by saying, "This is the work of a lifetime."

You will remember and forget, contracting and expanding on a daily basis, just like the opening and closing of your heart valve and the flow of your breath. One day you will be very clear, easily letting go of any story of struggle. Then the next day you may fall into a story that feels like it always has and always will have you in its grip. But remember, you are putting together the picture puzzle of your storyteller so you can unhook from its spells and every moment of relating *to* what you are experiencing rather than *from* it truly matters.

Once you see that you are in the meadow right now and it is only your cloud bank of struggle that keeps you from knowing it, you will become more and more curious, in a compassionate way, about whatever you are experiencing. You will also remember to turn your challenges over to Life, so the wisdom at the heart of Life can guide and support you. This will lead you to the place where you can simply be open to Life, entering its flow, knowing more and more ease and joy.

It is helpful to condense all that we have explored into what I call "The Four Lets" that will help you respond clearly and cleanly to whatever level of opening or closing is happening.

The Four Lets

- **Let Life**
- **Let It Be**
- **Let It Go**
- **Let Go**

Let Life is a doorway out of the core reactions of your storyteller through the art of turning your challenges over to Life, allowing the Intelligence of Life to support you every step of the way.

This opens you up into the curiosity of **Let It Be**, which is about not fighting what you are experiencing so in that spaciousness you can explore what is going on. This allows you to bring the healing of your compassionate attention to your spells, which helps them to let go.

In **Let It Go** you come to a place where you can simply let go of many of your spells when they arise. You have given them enough curiosity and compassion that they pass through you rather than getting caught in their stories.

This brings you to **Let Go** which is when your cloud bank of struggle has been thinned enough that you are able to rest in the meadow of your being. Opening to this moment, you relax into Life, allowing it to flow through you, as you.

If you look carefully, there is a progression of consciousness in the Four Lets starting with Let Life which helps immensely when you are caught in your storyteller and progressing all the way to Let Go where you are fully open to Life.

Let us take time to explore each in depth.

Let Life:

There will be many times in your life when reaction will take over so fast that you won't have a clue about what is going on inside of you. You will be caught in your storyteller, feeling there is no way out of the morass of feelings and stories that are flooding through you. There also will be times when you can see you are caught because you are tightening around a situation, but you don't know what is going on inside of you and you feel resistance to doing the *you-turn* and looking. Finally, there will be times where you use the tools of consciousness and your resistance only gets tighter.

When you are this contracted, it is very easy to get seduced into your spells: "I am not doing Life right." "This is going to last forever." "I am not enough." "What is wrong with me that this keeps on happening?"

When this happens, there will be an almost magnetic attraction to falling into them. It will feel as though most everything inside of you wants to buy into the spell, but if you have followed that path enough times in your life, you will remember that it only leads to more suffering.

This is the time to open into **Let Life**. The first gift that comes from **Let Life** is the art of acknowledging you are caught and feeling powerless in the face of the reactions inside of you. Rather than being completely lost in reaction, it is powerful to consciously acknowledge that you are caught. This may not seem like much, but it is a moment of consciousness within the clouds of spells. The ability to say, "I see that I am caught in reaction," allows you to take a half-step out of the morass of struggle.

The second part of **Let Life** is the willingness to ask Life for clarity. No matter how stormy the storyteller is, you have never left the meadow. It is always with you no matter what is happening in your life, and can be accessed simply by asking for help from the Intelligence that is Life.

Remember, this kind of asking isn't looking for an answer. That just keeps you caught in your head. To ask an open-ended question of Life such as, "What is asking to be met?" or "What is the way through this?" or "What am I ready to see?" creates an opening so that the answers can live themselves through you in Life's time and in Life's way. Every moment of asking counts, especially when it doesn't seem like anything is happening.

> -Ω- Allow one long, deep breath and contemplate the possibility that you are not living the dance of Life alone.

Let It Be:

As you awaken, there will be more and more moments where you become interested in what is going on inside of you when you are in reaction, contraction or just not available to Life. You become willing to do the *you-turn*, turning your attention toward yourself with the intention of allowing whatever is happening to be there. This is the next **Let** of **Let It Be**, and it is about not resisting what is happening so that your reactions can calm down. Then it becomes easier to see and become available to what is going on inside of you.

It is in this space of allowing things to be as they are that alchemy happens, for the truth of spells is that they are like people. If you try to fix them, deny them, judge them, or get rid of them, they resist you back. When you are willing to acknowledge the spells and listen to their world, they feel heard, and that dramatically increases the chances that, when you are ready to let go of a spell, it will let go!

The default mode of your storyteller, which is resistance, is the opposite of 'allowing' which is at the heart of Let It Be. But remember what we explored in Chapters Five and Six: if you try to get away from what you are experiencing, it only increases the struggle of your storyteller. If you turn toward it with curiosity, you now have some space around what you are experiencing, and it is spaciousness (the opposite of reaction) that heals.

Allowing is key here, for you can't really look and listen to something if you are resisting its presence. Allowing comes from the understanding that embedded in all of your reactions to Life are spells that need you and are waiting for your willingness to be with them so they can let go. One of the clearest ways to describe what we are talking about here is the ability to say, "For just this moment, I am going to allow whatever is happening inside of me to be there so I can bring my attention to it."

Allowing trusts that *Life is for Life*. Allowing knows that everything that tightens us is a growth opportunity. There is nothing to be afraid of or ashamed of. There is just something to be opened to, explored, and seen for what it is: blocked energy that makes up the spells. Allowing opens a door so you can show up for your own life experiences and give them the attention they need to let go.

Let's take anxiousness as an example. Imagine that this is a feeling you have known a lot in your life. Every time it appears, you feel resistant, overwhelmed and desperate to get out of this feeling. But if you are honest, whatever you do to get out of the feeling may bring temporary relief, but it doesn't bring the lasting freedom from anxiousness you long for. Through **Let It Be** you turn your attention toward it, being curious about whatever you are experiencing that causes you to say you are anxious. If you stay with this exploration, anxiousness itself will let go, and if it arises again, you will be less afraid of it, so it will pass through much more quickly.

Sometimes it is hard to access the power of letting something be. You have been so trained to resist and control. To accept your immediate experience so you can explore it, it helps to relate to this experience as if you have chosen it. Imagine what it would be like to have the flu and be miserable all day long. Then imagine shifting your relationship with it by saying, "I chose this as a part of my awakening. Rather than resisting it, I choose to be with it." With this kind of spaciousness, your experience of the flu would be completely different.

If that doesn't work, imagine that Life has chosen it for you, that this is where destiny has placed you, and your job is to bring your conscious attention to it. This allows whatever suffering you are experiencing to be transformed back into the free-flowing aliveness that is who you really are. Both of these shifts of perception take you out of the victim mode of unconsciousness and open you into the power of consciously looking at whatever you are experiencing, which is what **Let It Be** is all about.

-Ω- Pause for a moment and take in the last stanza of
the Beatles song "Let It Be:"
And when the night is cloudy,
There is still a light that shines on me,
Shine until tomorrow, let it be.
I wake up to the sound of music,
Mother Mary comes to me
Speaking words of wisdom, "Let it be."
Let it be, let it be, let it be, yeah, let it be.
There will be an answer, let it be.
Let it be, let it be, let it be, yeah, let it be.
Whisper words of wisdom, "Let it be."

Let It Go:

As you become more able to see your spells through the **first two Lets** of **Let Life** and **Let It Be**, it becomes easier to see and unhook from a spell when it arises. This brings you to **Let It Go**, which is the place where you soften around a spell and simply let it pass through you.

Let's take the feeling of being anxious again. Now that you have explored it through **Let It Be**, rather than identifying with the spell by saying, "I am anxious," you can see it as a pattern of belief that was conditioned inside of you. You then become able to say, "This is just anxiousness and I don't need to tighten around it." You are not interested in following the storyline of anxiety or resisting its energy. So you simply **Let It Go** and bring your attention back to Life. Remember, you are not the spells. They were just conditioned into you when you were young. Instead, you are that which can see the spells, and the more you watch them, the more they lose their power over you.

Sometimes it is difficult to let go of a spell, but the more you see the alchemy that happens when you bring your full attention to the bound up energy of a spell, the more you recognize that there is no spell that is worth closing around. If you do close, you can see clearly that in doing so you lock this spell inside and bind up your joy in the process. There comes a time when nothing is worth closing around. You want to stay open to Life more than you want to identify with the seductiveness of your spells.

Unhooking from a spell is one of the most joyous experiences of Life, and just a little bit of unhooking goes a long way. Yes, there is a very deep urge inside of you to tighten down around your spells. Make it a passion of your life to recognize your spells and relax, letting them pass through you rather than fighting them. You have been taught to identify with your spells for most of your life, so the tendency to get drawn in is strong, but the willingness not to be so enamored by the drama of the spells becomes stronger the more you develop your capacity for compassionate curiosity. As you let your life be about allowing whatever happens to make it through you, you will know your natural state of joy.

-Ω- Let go of reading and bring your attention to your breath. On the next in-breath tighten your muscles and on the out-breath, slowly let go. Do as many letting-go breaths as calls to you, and then smile.

Let Go:

All of our exploring together brings us to the **fourth Let** of **Let Go**, the joy of relaxing into Life. With **Let Go**, rather than trying to control or manipulate Life, you remember to stay open to it, to let go to it. You recognize that the great river of Life has been unfolding long before you came here and will continue on long after you have left. You also realize that Life happens. You don't make it happen. You learn to step back and bear witness to its unfolding. The way Pema Chodren defines awakening is appropriate here – "Relaxing into Life!"

Through **Let Life**, **Let It Be** and **Let It Go**, you thin enough of your cloud bank of spells so you discover the safety and the joy of being here for Life, not an idea of it but the living experience of it.

These two little words, **Let Go**, capture the essence of what this whole book is about, and they are a wonderful mantra for Life. With **Let Go**, you open to the natural unfolding of Life rather than using your mind to protect yourself from it. When you do start becoming tight, it becomes as simple as saying, "Let go," which dissolves whatever struggle your storyteller is caught in.

Instead of being open to Life, you were conditioned to be afraid of it, believing that your job was to control it and make it be what you thought it should be. This only causes you to live tight and small. You are so busy trying to make the next thing right that you can't be here with Life. If you are honest with yourself, you will see that trying to make the unknown known so you can stay in the illusion of control has never brought you the lasting peace you long for.

A Tibetan Lama told Andrew Harvey, author and teacher of mystic traditions, that once you see what is going on here, you will nearly die laughing. We have been trying to control the uncontrollable, keeping ourselves tied up in knots! We all have been like gnats on the back of an elephant trying to control the elephant and feeling very frustrated that it never quite works out. When you finally stop trying to control and instead show up for the ride, you discover that this is where the joy is. Even the greatest of challenges now open you back into the meadow of Life.

Instead of staying tight and small in a mind that is based on fear, it is time to expand and open, discovering that the safest thing you will ever do is show up for the Life you have been given. This can be scary, for you have been caught for a long, long time in a conceptual world, believing that your mind was in charge of Life. In giving it this impossible task, it has, like most minds, become self-absorbed and neurotic. It is not fun to be lost in the struggle of your storyteller, which focuses mainly on itself all day long. When you realize that Life is smarter than you, you can expand back into Life.

Most people, caught in their fear of Life, believe their minds are more powerful than Life. But I ask you, do you beat your heart? Did you create your eyes? Do you bring forth spring out of winter? Do you heal the cuts on your skin? No, the forces of Life create and orchestrate life, and Life is trustable. Yes, it includes death, illness and loss, but the suffering you experience by not trusting it, by not opening to it, is far greater than any pain you will experience as you stay open to it all, even to the difficult parts.

Upon discovering that Life is smarter than you and knows what it is doing, you no longer live exclusively in your mind. That doesn't mean that you don't use the mind, but it no longer uses you, keeping you cut off from Life by its endless game of struggle. Your mind is an exquisite tool to help you maneuver through your life, but thoughts about Life are not Life. Your mind's true function is to be fully here for Life, not to control it.

-Ω- Let go of reading for a few moments and simply open to Life. Recognize that whatever is happening right now has never happened on this planet before. It is totally brand new! Rather than thinking about it, just receive it. Drink it in. It is safe to let yourself go to the great river of Life.

You are homesick for this. You are homesick for fully participating in the great unfolding of Life that is happening right now as you are reading this book. Life is giving you the gift of Life and for this moment you get to bear witness to it. The flow of events that is your life is unique to you, and one day you won't be here to experience it anymore. Life will keep on unfolding, but you will be gone. Out of this recognition comes a passion to listen deeply to whatever your attention is drawn to in any moment - the song of a bird, a delicious meal, a pain in your belly, a person who is in joy, a person who is suffering, fear in your mind, your death – for *this is your life.*

In your passion for Life, you no longer want to resist the flow of events that is at the heart of **Let Go**. Instead, you allow more and more moments of the day to pass through you. Anthony de Mello, the Jesuit priest and psychotherapist, calls it "absolute cooperation with the inevitable." What gives Life its richness is the willingness to live it. Embrace it rather than resisting it. Live your life! Joy arises out of embracing every experience. The only way you can become this open is to realize that everything on this planet is impermanent, including the planet. People, animals, events, and experiences all die. It is natural for everything that appears to eventually disappear back into mystery. So be willing to die into Life!

The more you let go to Life, the more available you become. There arises an intimacy between you and Life. Rather than a series of problems to be solved, Life becomes a dance of discovery with the simplest of things having deeply profound effects on you. With great joy you discover that the more you are okay with what is, the more you see that everything is okay. There is a sense of ease and a willingness to let go of the part that is afraid of what will happen next.

Trusting this great mystery of Life, you are willing to be blind about the future. You realize that anything is possible and nothing is certain. You recognize that your mind can never know what is going to happen next, but that is okay, for you know the greatest gift a human can know: the ability to be with Life as it is right now! Instead of thinking and planning your way through Life, you discover how to feel for the energies. There are currents flowing through Life and you learn how to let these forces move you. In feeling your way through your life, your storyteller becomes quieter and your heart becomes the guiding force.

My book *The Magical Forest of Aliveness* is an exploration of the journey back to the meadow of Life that we have been exploring. It is a fairy tale for adults (although many people have told me their children love it, too) about a little girl named Rose who gets caught behind the walls of the village called 'Mind.' She eventually finds her way out of the village and back into the magical forest of aliveness where, in a beautiful clearing deep in the forest, she rediscovers who she really is. Then a lion, a tiger and a bear teach her about consciousness and how to be open to Life.

When it is time to go back to the village, her old fears suddenly rise up to the surface. "I can't be open to Life. That sounds like I will be doing nothing. Besides, I will just be a doormat! Either bad things will happen or nothing will happen." Now, however, Rose can feel how these thoughts are tightening her rather than opening her, and she is able to unhook from their stories.

As she looks across the field toward the village, the words 'don't know' come to her as a healing balm. When she was caught in the village of Mind, those words created fear and frustration, but now they come from her wisdom self. "I truly don't know what will happen in my life, and I don't need to know. My life will unfold the way it needs to. Having to know kept me caught in my head. Not needing to know keeps me open to the great mystery of Life."

> -Ω- Close your eyes for a few moments, allowing in a deep breath. Then on a long, slow out-breath, say, 'don't know.' Stretch the words out so they last for your whole out-breath. Breathe this 'don't know' breath as many times as it calls to you.

Through the **Four Lets**, we have been exploring the most important choice a human being has: how you use your mind. The choice is to use it to control or to connect. In fact, this is the only true choice you have. It is either mind or moment. You either give your attention to all the stories in your head that make up your storyteller or you allow your life to unfold, giving it your passionate and compassionate attention, interacting with it in a natural way. There will always be challenges, but Life is a lot easier when you relax into it enough so you dance with Life rather than living from your spells.

The Heart:

All that we have explored allows the wisdom of your heart, rather than your mind, to become the guiding force in your life. Life shows up differently when you discover how to listen to your heart. Remember in Chapter Seven when you were invited to imagine somebody you deeply love and you were able to see how the energy in your chest shifts? It expands, opens and even glows. You were also able to see that if you stayed with it long enough, your whole body would glow. Every cell in your body responds to the radiance of an open heart. So, too, do the different parts of yourself, your loved ones, strangers, plants and animals. They all thrive when touched by an open heart.

What does it look like when the heart is your guiding force? There is openness, for the heart doesn't divide and separate like the mind does. The words that describe a heart-focused Life are 'allowing,' 'spaciousness,' 'curiosity,' 'playfulness,' 'spontaneity' and 'trust.' As your mind drops into your heart, you value being real, speaking truth, not fighting what is, responding rather than reacting, being curious about what is, having times of quiet and stillness, not asserting your position, listening and appreciating your life just the way it is. And when you live a heart-oriented life, not only do you live and thrive from the meadow of your being, you also become a healing force in the world.

The more your mind gets enfolded by your heart, the more you begin to experience Life in ways that you have longed for: an ease in loving and being loved, the joy of seeing Love everywhere, and a deep gratitude for even the smallest of things. We have explored that the essence of our existence is Love, but because we don't see this, we are starving. We are like fish in the ocean thirsty for water, so our whole life becomes a search for Love. All you have to do is listen to the lyrics of most popular songs and you will hear how starved we are.

To discover the courage (which means 'of the heart') to look at your spells so they can thin, not only allows you to discover the power of your own heart, but also to recognize that the love affair you have longed for your whole life is with yourself! When you are able to open your heart to all of you, so that there is no spell, sensation, feeling or thought inside of you that cannot be included in your heart, then your body and mind will glow with the energy of Love.

No love from outside of you will ever fully satisfy you because the only way to relieve that longing is to know who you truly are. The love you receive from another human being is only a drop in the bucket in comparison to the depth of Love you can become when you realize you *are* Love! You arise from the energy that animates everything. Every atom that makes up every cell in your body is filled with light, and the activity of that light is Love. To step out of the struggles of your storyteller and rest in the field of Love is to experience the radiance that you truly are!

Then an amazing thing begins to happen. Rather than the suffering of endlessly searching for love, you begin to realize that the greatest joy of Life is to *be* this Love. In realizing that your destiny is to be Love, another wondrous shift begins to happen. You tap into the great circle of giving and receiving that is Love. The more you give Love, the more it comes back to you, and you recognize it everywhere.

This Love then expands out to include all of humanity. You recognize there is only one of us here and we are all in this together. You see that Life is like a mighty tree with billions of leaves. Each person is a leaf and we are all on the same tree, connected by the same roots and looking out of everybody's eyes is the same animating Presence that permeates all of Life.

Most people you meet don't see this about themselves and so they maneuver through Life caught in their spells. This causes their light to dim, but through the eyes of your heart you can see who they truly are. In a relatively new Christmas song called *Mary Did You Know?* there is a line that says "When you kiss your little baby, you kissed the face of God." It is wonderful to see the face of God in baby Jesus, but when you wake up to the truth of Love, you see the face of God in everyone!

When living from your heart, you are automatically open to everyone and you give them the fullness of your presence, whether it is a grocery store clerk, a person next to you in a traffic jam or your loved one. It doesn't matter how deeply caught they are in their spells. It doesn't matter that they, like all human beings, have done unskillful things in their lives and maybe even have hurt you in their unskillfulness. You realize that they are doing the best they know how while caught in the conditioning of their spells. Relating to them from your heart and allowing the truth of their being to shine out of your eyes helps to thin their storyteller. You then become a force of consciousness in the world.

This kind of Love also expands out to include all of Life. You recognize that the source of every single thing is the same: the Intelligent Presence at the heart of Life. Just as people are like leaves on the tree of Life, all nourished by the same source, so too is every single form! It doesn't matter whether it is a person, a feeling, a thought, a plant, an insect, a rock, grass, a dolphin, a star or your child. All are brought forth out of mystery and are animated by the same energy, and all deserve to be met with the spaciousness, the inclusion, the acceptance of the heart. This is when you step into your true essence: a lover of what is!

It does appear that there are separate forms, but you see the interconnectedness at the same time, for everything is linked to and nourished by the roots of the tree of Life, which is Love. Every single expression of Life is like a cell in your heart. Yes, the cell is a separate entity, but it would not exist without the community heart; and the heart would not exist without the greater community of a body; and the body would not exist without the whole community of Life!

When you live from the heart, you swim in a sea of gratitude, not taking anything for granted. You are grateful for everything: for the food that the Earth gives you every day and all of the forces it takes to make this happen; for the amazing gift of a body that allows you to experience Life through the senses; for your senses themselves (what would it be like to be unable to see or hear!); for the ability to walk (many people can't do this ever again). You even discover how to be grateful for the challenges of your life, for you recognize they are clearing your storyteller so you can be fully here for Life. There is practically no greater joy a human being can know than living from gratitude, and this naturally opens up when you see through your spells enough that you live from your heart.

Whether it is rivers, people, the seasons, your body or your challenges, the joy of seeing it all as the out-pouring of Love is indescribable, for it is coming home. When Life becomes something to love rather than to possess, you are moved beyond feeling separate and alone, for your heart weaves you back into the very fabric of Life. This then becomes your passion: to show up for Life and experience it through your heart. Everything else is secondary in relationship to this willingness to be available to Life with an open heart. And when you are cut off again, caught in your spells, you now know how to bring Love to them.

-Ω- See the Earth in your imagination and allow yourself to be moved by her beauty – the green of her mountains, the blue of the oceans, the gold of her fields. Now see the billions of people that are right now walking, driving, sleeping, working, birthing, dying, laughing, crying. See that most of them have clouds swirling around their head that block their view of Life. Now see a human being who has become free from her cloud bank standing in front of a person who hasn't, touching that person with her heart. Watch this heart energy dissipate the person's clouds so that he or she is again available to Life. Now see both of these people turning to two other people and meeting them with the healing of the heart. Watch this spread all over the Earth as more and more people come out of their cloud banks of struggle and live from the meadow of their being. Know that your life is a part of this healing process that is happening now on our planet.

Trusting the Process:

You don't have to try to find your heart, for it is always here. It has just been hidden because of the endless addiction to struggle that is your storyteller. Trying to find it is just more cloud bank. The healing you are ready for doesn't come from changing anything. It comes from the willingness to be curious about what is right now in a spacious way so your cloud bank can thin, and, *voilà*, there is the meadow of your own heart.

Yes, this takes patience, which is not a strong quality of the storyteller. The definition of patience is "quiet, steady perseverance; even-tempered care." As one of the teachers I highly respect once said, "The three most important words in awakening are 'Just keep walking'!"

For most of us, our awakening will be slow and steady, hardly noticeable in comparison to the noisy storyteller in our heads, but it is there none-the-less. It is similar to what happens at the beginning of the day; there isn't an instant appearance of light. Instead, it is a gradual shift from the dark of night to the first fingerlings of light on the horizon, to the stars slowly disappearing until the light of day fully appears.

So don't expect instant awakening, but know that Life is waking you up. If it wasn't, you wouldn't be interested in what is being offered here. Ramana Maharshi, one of the most respected teachers of awakening on this planet, once said that all you need is the willingness to awaken. Since you are reading this book, the willingness is already here. So no matter what your life looks like, Life is waking you up, step-by-step, out of the suffering of struggle and back into Life.

You can trust the flow of Life. It is for you. The same Intelligence that has shaped the unfolding of Life from the beginning of time – creating stars, forming the Earth and bringing you forth out of mystery – is what is breathing you right now. It is only one step more to recognize that the same Intelligent Creativity is in charge of the unfolding of your life. The meadow of your heart will not fail you. It is working tirelessly to bring you back step-by-step into recognition of who you truly are.

The more you trust Life, the more you show up for your own life. The most meaningful relationship you will ever have is your willingness to be in relationship with what Life is giving you. The more you are willing to be curious and accepting, the more you will discover that the path to your freedom is in the ground beneath your feet, for what is in the way, is the way. Be willing to be curious about what is right now and Life will guide you home. Then you will become the fullness of what human beings have been brought forth to experience: the consciousness that can celebrate and bear witness to the amazing creation called Life.

RE-MEMBERING SECTION

This week's Re-membering Statement:

I welcome Life as it is right now

Your Own Statement:

_____

Re-membering Session

You have spent nine weeks dipping the finger of your attention into the river of your experience, discovering how to meet yourself right where you are through quieting your mind and opening your heart. This session will include the standard pathway we have been developing, but if it calls to you, find your own this week. Whether you develop your own or stay with the pathway we have been exploring, we will then add one more step to this session. If timing your session, add one minute, taking it to fourteen minutes.

If you are going to create your own pathway, below is a list of the skills we have explored through the previous chapters. If you are called to use the standard pathway, skip this section and go to the paragraph on Page 200 that begins with "Let's begin."

In creating your own pathway, listen to yourself and discover what works best for you. Play with what calls to you. As you continue to give yourself the gift of daily quiet time, know that your pathway can live and breathe. One day you may stay with the circle of your breath the whole time. Another day you will be grounded and spacious enough that you hardly need to anchor on your breath. On another, it will interest you to explore what is drawing your attention away from your breath, and the next day, all you may be able to do is turn it over to Life. Always use your breath as your initial ground and then go from there.

You will find the new step we are adding this week in the paragraph that begins on the bottom of Page 200 and says, "At the end of your meditation."

- On your in-breath, tighten every muscle in your body. Then very slowly relax everything on your out-breath as you say the great sound of letting go, "Ahh!"

- Open to the letting in of the in-breath and the letting go of the out-breath. As you ride the waves of breath, say silently to yourself, "In...Out. Deep...Slow".

- Lengthen your out-breath by breathing in through your nostrils and then gently blowing out through your mouth. As you become comfortable with a longer out-breath, breathe in and out through your nostrils.

- As you ride the circle of your breath, whenever you find yourself paying attention to your storyteller again, notice if you are telling yourself stories about the past or the future. If your stories are about the past say, "Past". If you notice your stories are about the future, say "Future". Then bring your attention back to the circle of your breath. If you can't immediately see past or future or if you are just spacing out, say, "Story."

- Explore your body by bringing your attention to a familiar place of holding in your body. Rather than turning away from it, turn toward it, being curious about what is happening in this area. Sensations will reveal themselves through the light of your attention just like a Polaroid picture.

- Say "As Is" on the in-breath and "I'm here" on the out-breath, reminding yourself to embrace all the parts of your being so they can receive the nourishment of your compassionate attention.

- Bring your attention to the circle of your breath, saying the calming/focusing words, "In...Out; Deep...Slow; Calm...Ease; As is...I'm here."

- Discover your own set of words to say on the rhythm of your breath.

- Whenever you notice that you are no longer fully with your breath, notice what has captured your attention. Say to the feeling/sensation/story, "I see you," and then let it go, bringing your attention back to your breath.

- When your attention has drifted away from the circle of your breath, ask yourself, "What is asking to be seen?" If you notice a feeling/sensation/story, explore it with the finger of your attention. Say to whatever you are noticing, "I see you. It is okay that you are here. Tell me about your world." These words are inviting you to be fully with whatever is there without falling into it, giving it the healing of your own heart.

- Allow curiosity to be your ground so you can sit with feelings/sensations/stories that arise and let them pass right through you.

Let's begin:

- Close your eyes and dip the finger of your attention into the river of your experience, noticing what it is like to be you right now.

- For at least three in-breaths, tighten your muscles and then very slowly relax everything on your out-breath as you say the great sound of letting go, "Ahh!"

- For a few breaths, bring your attention to the circle of your breath, saying the calming/focusing words, "In...Out; Deep... Slow; Calm...Ease; As is...I'm here." Or, you can say, "As is...I'm here" by itself.

- Let go of paying attention to your breath and allow curiosity to be your ground, allowing feelings/sensations/stories to arise and pass through you.

- If you find your attention wandering, come back to the circle of your breath and stay with it as long as it feels right, even if it is the whole time. Trust where you are. The more you discover you don't need to control your experience, the greater the chances are that you will be able to expand your attention beyond your breath and be curious, allowing the energy of feelings/sensations/stories to move through you.

At the end of your meditation (for both the people who created their own pathway and the people who followed the standard pathway), open your eyes and fully receive this moment of your life. See it with new eyes as if you have never seen it before. All of the millions of moments of your life have brought you here and this moment will never be the same again. Drink it in. Let go of any filters between you and this living moment so you can rest in the great river of Life.

Note that fear may come. Your mind is afraid of letting go of control for it has forgotten that something else is in charge, that it is all made out of Love and every single experience is for you. Open to it and discover that this is the safest thing you will ever do, for this moment is your home.

When you are ready, open your eyes.

Abbreviated Version:

- Find your own pathway.

- At the end of your session, open your eyes and receive this moment of your life with new eyes.

Or

- Close your eyes and dip the finger of your attention into the river of your experience, noticing what it is like to be you right now.

- For at least three in-breaths, tighten your muscles and then very slowly relax everything on your out-breath as you say the great sound of letting go, "Ahh!"

- Bring your attention to the circle of your breath, saying the calming/focusing words, "In...Out; Deep...Slow; Calm...Ease; As is...I'm here." Or, "As is...I'm here" by itself.

- Let go of paying attention to your breath and allow curiosity to be your ground, allowing feelings/sensations/stories to arise and pass through you.

- If you find your attention wandering, come back to the circle of your breath for a few breaths and then open up the field of your attention again and be curious about what sits here right now.

- At the end of your session, open your eyes and receive this moment of your life with new eyes.

Re-memberings

- You will remember and forget, contracting and expanding on a daily basis just like the opening and closing of your heart valve, and the flow of your breath.

- Let Life is the art of turning your challenges over to Life, allowing the Intelligence of Life to support you every step of the way.

- Let It Be is all about not fighting what you are experiencing so in that spaciousness you can explore what is going on, bringing it the healing of your heart.

- In Let It Go you come to a place where you can simply let go of many of your spells when they arise. Make it a passion of your life to recognize your spells and let them pass through you.

- This brings you to Let Go where you relax into Life, allowing it to flow through you. Rather than using your mind to protect yourself from the natural unfolding of Life, you open to it.

- The more you let go to Life, the more available you become. Rather than a series of problems to be solved, Life becomes a dance of discovery.

- All that we have explored allows the wisdom of your heart to become the guiding force in your life. The words that describe a heart-focused life are 'allowing,' 'spaciousness,' 'curiosity,' 'playfulness,' 'spontaneity' and 'trust.'

- Your body will glow with the energy of Love when you are able to open your heart to all of you, so that there is no spell, sensation, feeling or thought inside of you that cannot be included in your heart.

- There is only one of us here, and we are all in this together. Life is like a tree with billions of leaves. Each person is a leaf on that tree, connected by the same roots, and looking out of everybody's eyes is the same animating Presence that permeates all of Life.

- Everybody and everything deserves to be met with the spaciousness, the inclusion, and the acceptance of the heart. This is when you step into your true essence: a lover of what is!

- Don't expect awakening to appear instantly, but know that Life is waking you up.

- You can trust the flow of Life. It is for you. The same Intelligence that has shaped the unfolding of Life from the beginning of time, creating stars, forming the Earth and bringing you forth out of mystery, is what is breathing you right now.

CHAPTER 11

Awakening for Life

Everything we have been exploring together – the truth of the meadow of your being, how your storyteller keeps you separate from what is truly going on here, and that you can live from the meadow when you recognize and see through the spells you took on – is all opening you again to the creative flow of Life. This is about saying "Yes" to Life. That doesn't mean that you sit down by the side of the road and let it run you over. It means that at your core you know that everything in your life is for you: it is not just a random series of events. Life is an intelligent process. It knows what it is doing and it is safe to open to it.

This brings you into full engagement with what is happening rather than staying caught in a conversation about Life. We could call it 'surrender,' but this doesn't mean being defeated. It is about finally giving up your war with what Life is bringing you! We could also call it 'humility,' but the dictionary misses its full meaning when it defines it as "lowliness, meekness, submissiveness." True humility is a state of great availability. From this kind of openness, you finally realize how smart Life is. This fosters a shift from the mind that tries to control to the heart that connects.

Can Life be trusted? Alan Watts, the celebrated philosopher, author and teacher once said, "…it appears as a vivid and overwhelming certainty that the universe, precisely as it is at this moment, as a whole and in every one of its parts, is so completely right, as to need no explanation or justification, beyond what it simply is." In other words, it is safe to open to Life!

To open to the way things actually are, rather than always trying to make Life be what you think it should be, is the most courageous and healing thing you can do. When you see through the game of struggle enough so that the veils between you and this living moment – this miraculous, incandescent moment –lift, you become a healing presence in the world. Moments of full connection with Life matter. In fact, they matter more than you can possibly know. They are what will heal our world!

The struggling mind has been the dominant force on this planet for too long. When it is in charge, people literally value feeling separate and thus buy into the world of fear, believing that the only way to work with Life is to be in control. We have all believed this so strongly that we are sure that if we don't control Life, we will die. This breeds conflict, efforting, blaming, anxiety, resistance, compulsions, defensiveness, one-upmanship and judgment.

Author and evolutionary cosmologist Brian Swimme speaks directly to how deeply the cloud bank of the mind has taken over most human beings and how important it is that we see through its game of struggle and open again to the amazing creative flow of Life. When he uses the word 'sacred,' he is referring to the recognition of the mysterious, magical creation that is unfolding in every moment of Life.

> Something very basic within the human body, the human mind, the human sensitivity has closed down. The sacred dimension has been lost sight of. Our way out of our difficulty is the journey into the universe as sacred. It is activating the sensitivity of the human that responds to the sacred dimension of the universe. It is a regeneration of the human spirit, enabling it once again to tremble with awe before these naked mysteries. What awaits us is the unfurnished eye…meaning seeing what is before us.

> We don't see what is before us. Our trouble as a species is that we don't know where we are. We don't know what surrounds us. We don't know what's about us. We don't know what we are about. The task is to initiate ourselves into the universe, into this enveloping mystery, a region of delight and excitement.

So the greatest mission you can undertake is to initiate yourself back into Life, to see what is before you, to live from the unfurnished eye. This means your awareness is no longer cluttered with the stories of struggle that make up the cloud bank around your head that we explored in the meadow metaphor. When your urge to struggle with Life has calmed down and instead you are willing to show up for the Life you have been given, you become a force of healing in the world. Wherever you go, you are here and a person who is truly here is a focal point of consciousness in this fairly unconscious world.

Humanity urgently needs more and more of us who are willing to open to Life. The collective mind of humanity is deeply caught in the cloud bank of a conceptual world view. All of the unskillful actions on our planet and the heartache that ensues come from human beings that are not here for Life. They are so caught in their cloud banks of struggle that they act from hatred, domination, greed, victimhood, violence and fear. They can become so lost in their struggles that they can destroy their lives and impact the lives of many other people too.

The suffering that is created by unconscious human beings is enormous. The Institute on Drug Abuse reports that 48 million people from the age of 12 and up have used prescription medication for non-medical reasons. That doesn't even include all of the rampant abuse of nonprescription drugs, alcohol, cigarettes, food, credit cards, etc. The fallout from being lost in our cloud banks of struggle also includes physical, mental, emotional and sexual abuse, along with all of the attempts to manage the pain of the abuse such as hoarding, self-cutting, and violence.

Let's not forget the many wars that are happening right now on our planet and all of the consequences that children, women and men are suffering. Then there is our planet with its soil, water and atmosphere polluted from our inability to see the sacredness of every single thing. Let's include your life too. You, like most people, are probably living in a chronic, low-grade stream of struggle that sometimes flares up into bigger struggles. Instead of feeling the joy of being alive, you feel the weight of it. You may even be experiencing some of the suffering we explored in the last paragraph.

No matter how much you are struggling with what is showing up in your life, there is a way out of the endless game of struggle, not only for you, but for all beings. In fact, this time of crisis on our planet, rather than being a break-down, is a time of breakthrough. It holds the possibility that you and many other human beings can finally recognize that who you really are is not the cloud bank of struggle. It is the meadow of well-being that is always with you.

Elisabet Sahtouris, an evolutionary biologist, shows through the butterfly story that this transformation is possible. She says that, relative to its size, the caterpillar is one of the most destructive beings on this planet. It can devour a whole tree branch in record time. Eventually it weaves a cocoon around itself and, within that structure, fulfills its destiny to dissolve into formless goo. Out of that goo begins to emerge the first cells of the butterfly. These cells are called imaginal cells and the goo (the old) tries to destroy them! Because of this threat, these new cells gather together into groups, and in that support, the butterfly is born.

This is our story. The caterpillar and its self-absorbed destruction represent the old kind of mind that humanity has been living in. The caterpillar is necessary in the creation of the butterfly, but there comes a time when it has to die for the butterfly to be born. The butterfly, which represents the new kind of mind, is the opposite of the caterpillar. It doesn't destroy Life. Instead, it serves Life by pollinating flowers. It can also fly far and wide, so its view is much broader than that of the caterpillar. As we grow into our 'butterflyness,' we too can have a view that includes everything.

So know that, no matter what is happening in your life, you are an imaginal cell. You are a part of the shift from separation to connection that is happening on our planet, and your life matters. It makes a difference how you choose to be with your life. I love to say that the oceans are made out of drops of water. Which drop isn't important? You are a drop of water in the ocean of awakening consciousness that is now happening. And your actions count. Or as Desmond Tutu, the South African activist who won the Nobel Peace Prize once said, "Do your little bit of good where you are. It is those little bits of good put together that overwhelm the world." Yes, do good actions, but the most important action you can take is to heal the war inside of you. Have the courage to show up for what Life is showing you and follow the path home to your heart.

As you clear the pathway from unconsciousness to consciousness for yourself, you also are clearing it for the world. Every moment you relate to what Life is offering you rather than from it, every moment where you are curious about what is unfolding rather than trying to control it, every moment you meet yourself and all beings with the spaciousness of your aware heart, every moment you recognize that what's in the way IS the way, and every moment you reconnect with the pure joy of being alive, you become a healing presence in the world. Or, as Einstein once said, "There are only two ways to live your life: one is as though nothing is a miracle; the other is as though everything is a miracle."

-**Ω**- Let us use our imaginations to open up to this new era of possibility on our planet. In your imagination, see the Earth as completely dark. Now see that a few thousand years ago, a light turns on somewhere on the planet: the light of an awake heart. As the years unfold, see more and more lights turning on, as more and more hearts wake up. See these individual lights beginning to create a web of light all over the planet that shines into the pockets of darkness that still exist. Then see this all unfolding to a place where our planet fully shines, without one molecule of existence excluded from the healing of the heart.

This is possible and you are an essential part of this healing. How you live your life matters!

I would like to end by bringing us back to the last paragraph of the introduction:

For all the people that live on this beautiful blue-green jewel that is our planet, I thank you for your willingness to bring this process into your life. This gratitude comes from knowing that, as you discover and live from your field of well-being, your life will be transformed. It will also transform the lives of everyone you meet or even think about for the rest of your life. For when you are not caught in the world of struggle, you are here, open to the amazing majesty and mystery of Life, radiating presence and well-being. And human beings who have discovered how to be here, become an invitation to everyone they meet to unhook from the mind's addiction to struggle and open back into the joy of being fully here for Life.

For your healing and the healing of all beings, Life is bringing you home.

Spells

Below is the list of the eight spells we explored in the book and the different ways your storyteller can say them in your head. Check off the stories that you are familiar with and you will have a greater sense of the world of your storyteller. At the end of the list we put the spells in a circle so you can see that they are a circular-continuum.

Foundational Spells:

1. I am separate
____Life is only what you see

____There is me in here and life out there

____I am my thoughts

____I am this mind-made-me

2. Life is not safe
____Life rejects me

____Life abandons me

____It over takes me

____There won't be enough

____There will be too much

____It is hard

____I can't trust life

____I must run away/hide

____Life happens to me

____It is overwhelming

____There is no protection

____Life is dangerous

____Something bad will happen

____Life is not fair

____Life will not support me

____I can't count on anything

Operational Spells:

3. I must control Life

___I must resist what I don't like

___I must *do* Life

___I must hold onto what I do like

___I create my reality

___I've got it together

___I am in charge

___I won't......

___I am the best

___I will do it later

___Get over it

___It's no big thing

___I can control how others feel about me

___I need to understand

___I will hurt you

___I need to be prepared

___I will not look at what I am experiencing

___I must get to my goal

___I must control you

___You are the cause of my problems

___My life needs to be different

___I need to be different

___'It' is my responsibility

___You need to be what I need you to be

___I will be happy when....

___The love I want comes from outside of me

___You will not control me

___It is your fault

___I'm the only one who can take care of me

___I don't want to be seen

4. **I must do it right**

   ___I must be perfect

   ___I must be cool/together

   ___I must be on top of it

   ___I can't be authentic

   ___I am doing it right

   ___It is not okay to make a mistake

   ___I have to be right

   ___I will be what others need me to be

   ___I am better than you

   ___I must please you

   ___I won't be wrong

   ___I have to be best

   ___I must find the right answer

   ___My life will be over if I don't....

   ___I can't look stupid

   ___If I....I'll get into trouble

   ___I have to do it all myself

5. **I am not doing it right**

   ___I am too much

   ___I am less than

   ___I am going to do it wrong

   ___Everybody else does it right

   ___It's my fault

   ___I sabotage myself

   ___I am lazy

   ___I am a procrastinator

   ___I don't know how

   ___I am not trying hard enough

   ___I should have done it differently

   ___I am on the wrong path

_____I am wasting time

_____'It' is not working

_____I look foolish

_____I am scared

_____This is taking too long

_____I am wasting time

_____I didn't live up to their expectations

_____I am boring

_____I should have done it earlier

_____I don't look good/right

_____I can't concentrate/focus

_____I make too many mistakes

_____I didn't get what everybody else got

_____I don't know how to do my life

_____I don't perform the way they want me too

_____I should be happy/grateful

_____This will keep on happening

Hidden Spells:

6. **I am wrong**
   _____I am worthless

   _____I am bad/evil

   _____I am stupid

   _____I am a failure

   _____I don't belong

   _____I won't be able to ever get it together

   _____I am wrong to my core

   _____I am a fake

   _____I am a looser

   _____I can't change

_____I can't change things

_____I hate myself

_____I didn't live up to my potential

_____I hate what I am doing

_____I have no value

_____I am a mistake

_____I am helpless

_____I am inadequate

_____I've got to do 'it' better

_____It's not okay to feel what I feel

_____Life is out to get me

_____I will be found out

_____I don't deserve to be happy

_____I have run out of time

_____I missed my chance

_____I get what I deserve

_____I can't figure anything out

_____I don't fit in

_____I am not what others want me to be

_____Everyone else has it together

7. **I am not lovable**

_____I don't matter

_____I don't deserve this

_____I am not worthy

_____I will be rejected

_____Nobody will take care of me

_____Nobody likes me

_____I am not good enough

_____Nobody chose me

_____I don't deserve to exist

___I have no value

___I'll never feel loved

___They don't really love me

8. I am all alone

___This is all there is

___Despair is all there is

___This will last forever

___I am depressed

___I am lonely

___I don't know who I am

___Things will never change

___I feel left out

___I don't exist

___I don't want to live

___I will never get what I need

___There is no way out

___I am invisible

___Nothing is real

___I can't do this anymore

___I don't want to do this anymore

___I am trapped

___There is no space for me

___I don't fit in

___No one else cares if I live or die

___No one is here for me

___Everybody rejects me

___There is no hope for me

___I need to leave to make it safe

The Circle of Spells

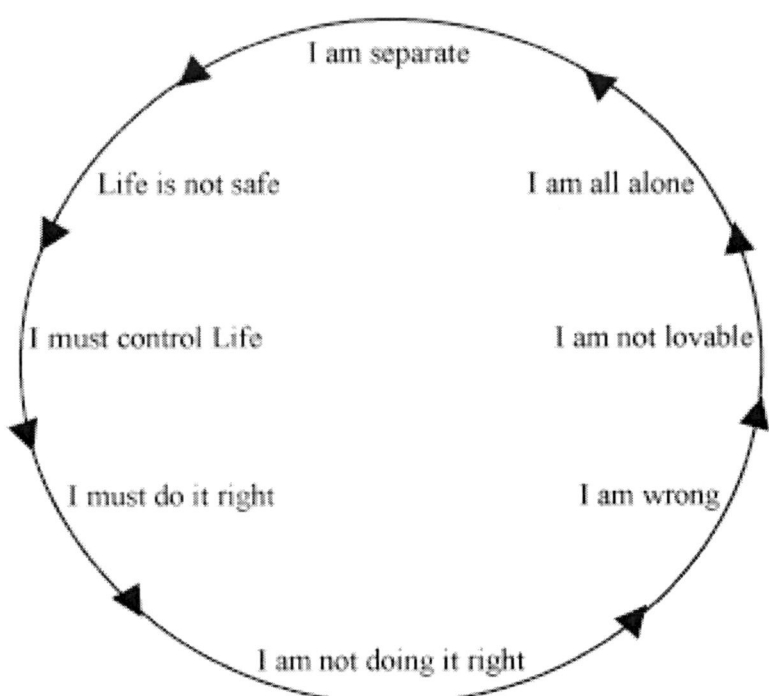

I am separate

Life is not safe

I am all alone

I must control Life

I am not lovable

I must do it right

I am wrong

I am not doing it right

Mary O'Malley
Author

Mary O'Malley is a speaker, author, group facilitator and counselor in private practice in Kirkland, Washington. For over 30 years she has explored and practiced the art of being truly present for Life. Through her organization, *Awakening,* she invites others into a center of clarity, compassion and trust that can be accessed no matter what is happening in their lives. She offers an invitation to live from the place in which the impossible becomes possible and our hearts soar with the joy of being alive.

Mary offers speaking engagements, retreats, workshops, phone and in-person counseling and phone and in-person groups.
To contact Mary:

awaken@maryomalley.com   www.maryomalley.com

Follow Mary on Facebook, Twitter, and her Blog by clicking on the links on her website homepage.

MarySue Brooks
Editor, Layout and Cover Design

MarySue has been working with Mary O'Malley since 1999 and it has truly been a partnership of awakening together. They have done meditation retreats, both group and personal, and have followed the vision of this work as it has unfolded in amazing ways.

They met in 1990 when MarySue was the Executive Secretary and Program Director at Unity of Bellevue. In her work there, she grew spiritually and in her computer and organizational skills. She later worked with a graphic designer where she learned the ins and outs of the Adobe Creative Suite. MarySue says, "It is my joy to support this work in every way I can."

Mary's Other Books
available through www.maryomalley.com
Amazon.com, Barnes & Noble, and local bookstores

The Gift of Our Compulsions
Published by New World Library, 2004

The Magical Forest of Aliveness
Published by Awaken Publications, 2009

Belonging to Life: The Journey of Awakening
Published by Awaken Publications, 2002 & 2011

CPSIA information can be obtained at www.ICGtesting.com
Printed in the USA
BVOW07s0052040814

361544BV00001B/58/P